Junior
MASTERCHEF
1994

Junior

19 94

MASTERCHEF

Junior MASTERCHEF 1994

FOREWORD BY LOYD GROSSMAN

VERMILION
LONDON

First published 1994

13 5 7 9 10 8 6 4 2

Compilation copyright © Union Pictures 1994
Recipes © The Contributors 1994
Foreword © Loyd Grossman 1994
Introduction © Richard Bryan 1994
Photographs © BBC Enterprises Ltd 1994
Front Cover Photograph © Richard Farley 1994

First published in the United Kingdom in 1994 by Vermilion
an imprint of Ebury Press, Random House, 20 Vauxhall Bridge Road, London SW1V 2SA

Random House Australia (Pty) Limited
20 Alfred Street, Milsons Point, Sydney,
New South Wales 2061, Australia

Random House New Zealand Limited
18 Poland Road, Glenfield
Auckland 10, New Zealand

Random House South Africa (Pty) Limited
PO BOX 337, Bergvlei, South Africa

Random House UK Limited Reg. No. 954009

A CIP catalogue record for this book is available from the British Library

ISBN: 0 09 178691 6

Junior MasterChef 1994
A Union Pictures production for BBC North

Series devised by Franc Roddam
Executive Producers: Bradley Adams and Richard Kalms
Producer and Director: Richard Bryan
Associate Producer: Glynis Robertson
Production Co-ordinator: Melanie Jappy

General Editor: Janet Illsley
Design: Clive Dorman
Recipes edited by: Susan Fleming
Front cover photograph: Richard Farley
Inside photographs: Huw Williams
Food Stylists: Jane Charlton and Valerie Berry

Typeset by Clive Dorman & Co. Ham, Surrey
Printed and bound in Great Britain by Clays Limited, St Ives plc.

Papers used by Ebury Press are natural recyclable products made from wood grown in sustainable forests.

Contents

Foreword

Viewers write into television programmes and their letters are read *and* taken seriously. Every programme postbag is a mix of praise and complaint, but few postbags are as surprising and informative as the one which arrives at the MasterChef office. Viewers have castigated my ties, excoriated my accent and sometimes deprecated my sense of humour. More happily – for me at least – I have also been advised on the best way to grow sorrel, educated in the intricacies of flour milling and given numerous tips about pubs, restaurants and hotels around Britain. Some viewers have even invited me 'round for dinner. Almost from the beginning of the series in 1990, viewers were suggesting a MasterChef programme for younger cooks.

The team and I were excited by the idea and began work immediately. It was a five year long, often frustrating, but always exciting process that brought us and twenty-seven young contestants to the television studios earlier this year. From the very beginning of our discussions everyone involved was determined that Junior MasterChef should differ as little as possible from the senior programme. Guest chefs and judges would be of the same stature as always – indeed some of our guests had already appeared on MasterChef – and judging would be rigorous. The famous red, yellow and blue kitchens would remain. The only concessions to youth were the demand for two courses rather than three; the setting of cooking time at one and a half hours and a rather more youthful budget of just £10.

As with MasterChef, everything depended on our assumption that our contestants would cook wonderfully well and perform fearlessly when the studio dates arrived. Needless to say I was just a tiny bit nervous. Thankfully I didn't have to be: by the time we were halfway into recording our first show there were smiles all round.

If you've seen any of the programmes you will know that the cooks were enthusiastic and inventive. You may also have noticed that most of them were good all rounders too, including a surprising number of excellent young musicians. The cooking was first rate – the best of our Juniors certainly cooked at MasterChef standard and the rest weren't too far away. Their cooking was different though. To begin with these contestants were much more at ease with the internationalisation of cooking: they were quite clearly young people who had grown up in a society where Indian, Chinese and American food were part of the currency of everyday eating. Exotic flavours and ingredients held no terror for them. Even more importantly they were completely relaxed around food. Good food wasn't a status symbol or a social statement; as far as they were concerned it was simply something to be enjoyed whether you were cooking it, serving it or eating it. And that's something that all cooks – young or old, amateur or professional – should remember.

I'm sure that many of our Junior contestants will appear on MasterChef when they're old enough, but I don't feel that Junior MasterChef is in any way a staging post towards MasterChef or any other competition. The enthralling performances of our young cooks has established Junior MasterChef as a sparkling and entertaining competition in its own right. This book is dedicated to our 1994 contestants with gratitude and affection.

Loyd Grossman

Notes for Recipe Users

Quantities are given in metric and imperial measures. Follow one set of measurements only, not a combination, because they are not interchangeable.

All spoon measures are level.

Fresh herbs are used unless otherwise stated.

Size 2 eggs are used unless otherwise suggested.

Ovens must be preheated to the temperature specified in the recipe.

All recipes serve 2.

Introduction

The recipes featured in this book are those of the twenty-seven young cooks who were selected to represent their regions in the first ever Junior MasterChef.

These contestants who reached the televised finals had all worked incredibly hard. Selected on the basis of their application forms, they had all won through at 'cook-offs' held in the unfamiliar atmosphere of a local catering college; they had devised, practised and written out the recipes for three complete menus – after all, any one of them might have reached the final; they had even supplied detailed timings of what they were going to do when; and they had stayed cool and calm with stars such as Danny Baker, Gary Rhodes and Michel Roux plus, of course, Loyd watching them work.

How things have changed for young cooks over the past years. Many of the ingredients which are now commonplace would not have been heard of when I was fifteen, and today most of them are available at the local supermarket. Wild mushrooms, sun-dried tomatoes, mascarpone and almost every herb and spice you can think of make regular appearances. And a blowtorch is an almost obligatory part of the batterie-de-cuisine!

During many a 'judgely huddle', celebrities who had previously taken part in MasterChef, commented that the dishes they had just tasted would have been equally at home in the adult competition. All the judges went away amazed by the talent shown by our young cooks.

We always felt certain that there would be many a 10 to 15 year old with ambitions in the kitchen well beyond fish fingers and baked beans. But never in our wildest dreams did we anticipate dishes like some of those you will discover in this book. We all hope that you will enjoy preparing, and above all, tasting them as much as the judges and our hungry television crew have done.

Richard Bryan
Producer and Director
Junior MasterChef

REGIONAL HEATS
The Midlands

Contestants
Miranda Tetley • Clare Engel • Lily Williams

Panel of Judges
Gary Rhodes • Ulrika Jonsson • Loyd Grossman

WINNER

Miranda Tetley's Menu

MAIN COURSE
Beef Olives in an Onion and Herb Sauce
"Full of flavour... confidently spiced beef olives" **Loyd**
"This one really excites me!" **Gary Rhodes**
Parmesan-baked Parsnips and Artichokes
Creamy Mashed Potatoes
Carrot Sticks and Broccoli Florets

DESSERT
Hot Chocolate and Brandy Mousse

Miranda Tetley is 15 years old and comes from Harby in Leicestershire. Miranda nominates 'eating out' as her favourite hobby, but playing the flute comes a close second. She's also a keep fit enthusiast, and regularly uses the gym at Ratcliffe College. One of her less strenuous pastimes is creating intricate designs from pressed flowers.

BEEF OLIVES IN AN ONION AND HERB SAUCE

6 thin slices Aberdeen Angus sirloin
   beef, about 150 g (5 oz) total weight
salt and freshly ground black pepper
olive oil for frying

Marinade:
30 ml (2 tbsp) extra-virgin olive oil
5 ml (1 tsp) golden syrup
juice of ½ lemon
3 spring onions, finely chopped
15 ml (1 tbsp) chopped parsley
leaves from 1 rosemary sprig, chopped

Stuffing:
25 g (1 oz) butter
4-5 spring onions, chopped
50 g (2 oz) mushrooms, sliced
chopped thyme and parsley leaves, to
   taste
fresh breadcrumbs from 2 small slices
   of granary bread

Sauce:
15 ml (1 tbsp) vegetable oil
1 medium onion, finely sliced
1 handful button mushrooms, finely
   chopped
1 clove garlic, finely chopped or crushed
leaves from 4 thyme sprigs
300 ml (½ pint) vegetable stock
5 ml (1 tsp) Dijon mustard
5 ml (1 tsp) tomato purée
5 ml (1 tsp) cornflour, blended with a
   little milk or water

To Garnish:
finely chopped parsley

1 Season the beef slices with salt and pepper and place in a shallow dish. Mix the marinade ingredients together, pour over the beef and turn the slices to coat evenly. Cover and leave to marinate overnight in the refrigerator.

2 To prepare the stuffing, melt the butter in a heavy-based frying pan and gently fry the spring onions for a minute or two. Add the mushrooms to the pan, keep stirring, then add the thyme leaves, chopped parsley, breadcrumbs, and salt and pepper. Fry gently for a few minutes. Transfer to a bowl.

3 Remove the beef slices from the marinade. Divide the stuffing equally between the slices of beef. Roll each one up and secure with a cocktail stick.

4 Heat a little olive oil in a frying pan, add the beef olives and brown rapidly on all sides. Transfer to a warmed oven-proof dish, cover and place in a preheated oven at 200°C (400°F) mark 6 while making the sauce.

5 Heat the oil in a pan and fry the onion until softened, but not browned, stirring from time to time. Add the mushrooms, garlic, thyme leaves, stock, mustard, tomato purée and a little salt and pepper. Bring to the boil, lower the heat and simmer for 2 minutes.

6 Pour the sauce over the beef olives, cover tightly with foil and cook in the middle of the oven for 1 hour. About 10 minutes before the end of cooking, stir in the blended cornflour to thicken the sauce. Taste and adjust the seasoning.

7 Remove the cocktail sticks from the beef olives and serve garnished with finely chopped parsley.

COOK'S TIP
This dish can take longer cooking without coming to any harm: just keep an eye on the sauce, to ensure that it does not evaporate too much. Top up with stock if necessary.

PARMESAN-BAKED PARSNIPS AND ARTICHOKES

2 parsnips, peeled and sliced
2 or 3 Jerusalem artichokes, peeled and sliced
salt
150 ml (¼ pint) single cream
15 g (½ oz) freshly grated Parmesan cheese
freshly grated nutmeg

1 Parboil the parsnips and artichokes in lightly salted boiling water for 5 minutes. Drain well and place in an ovenproof dish.

2 Mix the cream and Parmesan together and pour over the vegetables. Grate nutmeg over the top.

3 Cook in a preheated oven at 200°C (400°F) mark 6 for 30-40 minutes, until nicely browned. Serve hot.

JERUSALEM ARTICHOKES

Jerusalem artichokes look rather like knobbly potatoes but don't be misled – they have a very distinctive flavour of their own. Cut off the knobbly parts, then use a potato peeler to remove the skin. Immerse in cold water with a little lemon juice added to prevent discolouration, until ready to cook.

HOT CHOCOLATE AND BRANDY MOUSSE

55 g (2¼ oz) butter
1 dessertspoon brandy
75 g (3 oz) Terry's Plain chocolate,
* broken into pieces*
40 g (1½ oz) caster sugar
50 ml (2 fl oz) water
2 free-range eggs (size 3), separated
good pinch of ground cinnamon

1 Place a large roasting tin containing a 5 cm (2 inch) depth of water in a preheated oven at 200°C (400°F) mark 6.

2 Grease a 600 ml (1 pint) soufflé dish with 5 ml (1 tsp) butter and put the brandy in the bottom.

3 Put the chocolate pieces into a small heatproof bowl, add the rest of the butter and melt over a saucepan of simmering water. Still over the hot water, stir in the sugar together with the water. Keep stirring until smooth.

4 Remove from the heat and transfer the mixture to a larger bowl. Stir in the egg yolks and cinnamon. In another bowl, whisk the egg whites to a fairly stiff consistency and then carefully fold into the chocolate mixture.

5 Pour into the buttered soufflé dish and stand in the hot water in the roasting tin. Cook in the preheated oven for 30-40 minutes. Serve immediately, with pouring cream.

COOK'S TIP

Make sure you use a classic straight-sided soufflé dish for this dessert and butter it thoroughly, especially around the rim, to encourage the mixture to rise during baking.

REGIONAL HEATS
The Midlands

Contestants
Miranda Tetley • Clare Engel • Lily Williams

Panel of Judges
Gary Rhodes • Ulrika Jonsson • Loyd Grossman

Clare Engel's Menu

MAIN COURSE
Salmon and Plaice Twists with a Smoked Salmon
and Coriander Sauce

New Potatoes

Mangetouts

DESSERT
Halva and Pistachio Ice Cream with Raspberry Coulis and
Danish Nut Crisps

"This is fab!" **Ulrika Jonsson**

Clare Engel from Chapel Brampton in Northampton is
14 years old. Clare is a pupil at the Northampton
High School for Girls where ballet is probably her
favourite subject. The Engels are a family of talented skiers,
and always enjoy their annual visit to the French Alps.
Clare also plays the classical guitar and is a member of a
Spanish-style quartet.

SALMON AND PLAICE TWISTS WITH A SMOKED SALMON AND CORIANDER SAUCE

125 g (4 oz) salmon fillet, cut into
   4 long strips
125 g (4 oz) plaice fillet, cut into
   4 long strips
15-30 ml (1-2 tbsp) melted butter
salt and freshly ground white pepper

Sauce:
75 g (3 oz) butter
15 ml (1 tbsp) freshly chopped
   coriander
2 courgettes, sliced into julienne strips
⅓ cucumber, sliced into julienne strips
juice of ½ lemon
8 small strips smoked salmon

1 To make the salmon and plaice twists, twist the long strips of salmon fillet and plaice fillet together and secure with cocktail sticks at both ends. Place on a baking tray lined first with a large piece of foil, then with non-stick baking parchment.

2 Brush the twists with melted butter and sprinkle with salt and pepper. Fold over the foil to make a loose parcel. Bake in a preheated oven at 160°C (325°F) mark 3 for 15 minutes.

3 Meanwhile make the sauce. In a heavy-based pan, melt the butter, then add the coriander, salt and pepper. Stir well. Add the courgettes and cucumber, and simmer for 3 minutes.

4 Remove from the heat and add the lemon juice and smoked salmon. Spoon over the salmon and plaice twists, and serve immediately, with new potatoes and mangetouts.

COOK'S TIP

To make the twists, you will find it easier if the salmon and plaice strips are approximately the same length and thickness.

HALVA AND PISTACHIO ICE CREAM WITH RASPBERRY COULIS

3 eggs
25 g (1 oz) caster sugar
150 ml (¼ pint) whipping cream
125 g (4 oz) halva
25 g (1 oz) shelled pistachio nuts,
  coarsely chopped

Raspberry Coulis:
125 g (4 oz) raspberries, fresh or
  frozen
caster sugar, to taste

To Serve:
Danish Nut Crisps (see right)

1 Whisk the eggs and sugar together in a bowl until pale, thick and creamy; the mixture should have the consistency of whipping cream. It will take about 5 minutes to reach this stage.

2 Whip the cream in another bowl until it holds soft peaks. Using your fingertips, crumble the halva into the cream, then gently fold in.

3 Line the bottom of 2 ramekin dishes with some of the chopped pistachios. Add the rest to the cream mixture, along with the whisked egg mixture. Fold gently together, then spoon into the ramekins and level the tops. Place in the freezer for 1¼ hours.

4 To make the raspberry coulis, purée the raspberries in a food processor. Add sugar to taste. Pass through a nylon sieve to get rid of any pips, then chill in the refrigerator until needed.

5 Turn the ice creams out of the ramekins on to chilled serving plates and surround with the raspberry coulis. Serve with Danish Nut Crisps.

DANISH NUT CRISPS

45 g (1¾ oz) butter
40 g (1½ oz) caster sugar
1.25 ml (¼ tsp) vanilla essence
50 g (2 oz) self-raising flour
1.25 ml (¼ tsp) bicarbonate of soda
shelled pistachio nuts, to finish

1 Work the butter into the sugar in a bowl using a wooden spoon, or blend together in a mixer or food processor. When the sugar has been incorporated, add the vanilla essence. Sift in the flour and bicarbonate of soda.

2 Mix gently to form a smooth dough, but do not overwork. Roll the mixture into balls, the size of large cherries. Arrange on ungreased baking sheets, leaving room for the biscuits to spread during cooking. Top each one with a pistachio nut.

3 Bake in a preheated oven at 180°C (350°F) mark 4 for 10 minutes or until golden brown. Leave on the baking sheets for a few minutes, then transfer to a wire rack to cool.

HALVA

A popular confection in Greece and Turkey, halva is available from delicatessens and larger supermarkets in this country. It is made from crushed sesame seeds or almonds combined with a boiled sugar syrup.

Contestants

Miranda Tetley • Clare Engel • Lily Williams

Panel of Judges

Gary Rhodes • Ulrika Jonsson • Loyd Grossman

Lily Williams' Menu

MAIN COURSE

Roast Pheasant on a bed of Apple and Quince
Potatoes, Carrots and Broccoli

DESSERT

Blackberry Mousse, served with Langue de Chat Biscuits

"Sensational!" **Loyd**

From Oxford, 14 year old Lily Williams was the first televised Junior MasterChef cook. She is a pupil at the Cherwood Upper School. Like most of the Oxford undergraduates, Lily gets around town on her trusty bike, which takes her between assignments as a reporter for the school magazine. At home the Williams' family are deeply involved in 'Green Issues' and Lily is doing her bit for self-sufficiency by keeping chickens.

ROAST PHEASANT ON A BED OF APPLE AND QUINCE

1 pheasant, plucked and cleaned
45 ml (3 tbsp) olive oil
1 medium onion, sliced
3 crisp medium apples (Blenheim or
    Cox), peeled, cored and sliced
3 garlic cloves, halved
75 g (3 oz) quince paste
25 g (1 oz) butter
salt and freshly ground black pepper
2 bacon rashers

To Serve:
thin gravy

1 Heat 15 ml (1 tbsp) of the oil in a pan, add the onion and fry gently until lightly softened. Add the apple slices, garlic and quince paste. Turn into a deep baking tray and drizzle the remaining oil evenly over the surface. Place the pheasant on top.

2 Cut the butter into small pieces and smear over the pheasant. Season lightly. Cover with the bacon. Place in a preheated oven at 200-220°C (400-425°F) mark 6-7 and roast for 45-60 minutes until the pheasant is tender. Baste three or four times during cooking.

3 Transfer the pheasant to a large warmed serving dish. Cover and leave to stand for 5 minutes. Scoop out the apple mixture from the tray and put in a blender or food processor. Purée, then pass through a sieve into a warmed serving bowl.

4 Pour the gravy over the bird and serve it surrounded by potatoes and steamed vegetables, such as carrots and broccoli. Serve the apple and quince purée separately.

QUINCE PASTE

The quince belongs to the same family as the apple and pear but is not eaten raw. It is probably best known for the fragrant paste made by cooking the fruit slowly with sugar. Quince paste is available from delicatessens.

BLACKBERRY MOUSSE

450 g (1 lb) fresh blackberries
125 g (4 oz) caster sugar
juice of 1 small lemon
2 gelatine leaves
2 egg whites

1 Place the blackberries, sugar and lemon juice in a heavy-based pan and simmer gently for about 10 minutes. Pass through a nylon sieve, pressing as much pulp through as possible, using a wooden spoon.

2 Put the gelatine leaves in a bowl and just cover with cold water. Leave for 2 minutes to soften. Warm the blackberry purée gently in a pan, then add the gelatine. Stir until the gelatine has dissolved. Leave the mixture until it is just beginning to set.

3 Whisk the egg whites until they form soft peaks, then fold this into the purée.

4 Transfer the mousse to individual serving dishes. Chill in the refrigerator until set, about 1-1½ hours.

5 Serve with Langues de Chat biscuits.

LANGUES DE CHAT

50 g (2 oz) butter
50 g (2 oz) caster sugar
2 egg whites
50 g (2 oz) plain flour, sifted
vanilla essence

1 Cream the butter and sugar together well until light and fluffy. Whisk the egg whites lightly and gradually beat into the creamed mixture. Carefully fold in the flour and a little vanilla essence to taste.

2 Place in a piping bag fitted with a 1 cm (½ inch) plain nozzle, and pipe into 7.5 cm (3 inch) lengths on a greased and floured baking sheet.

3 Bake in a preheated oven at 200°C (400°F) mark 6 for 10 minutes. The biscuits should be pale golden in colour, a little darker around the edges. Transfer to a wire rack to cool.

Makes 20-24

Contestants
Katie Targett-Adams • Lindsay Craig • Rosemary Morrison

Panel of Judges
Lady Claire Macdonald • Craig Charles • Loyd Grossman

WINNER

Katie Targett-Adams' Menu

MAIN COURSE

Chicken Breast filled with Sun-dried Tomato and Fresh Basil
wrapped in Aubergine, on a Tomato Salsa

"Oh! It's delicious!" **Lady Claire Macdonald**

Potato and Parsnip Purée

Crispy Noodle Nest filled with Cucumber Ribbons and Sesame Seeds

DESSERT

Apple and Lemon Sorbet on a Blackcurrant Coulis,
with Hazelnut Heart Biscuits

Katie Targett-Adams is 14 years old and lives in Edinburgh. Katie attends St George's School where her favourite subject is Art. She has recently completed an impressive course-work project which involved constructing huge fruit and vegetables from unusual fabrics. Together with several of her friends, Katie will soon be off to America to perform the School production of 'The Little Prince'. Katie also plays the clarsach, a small Scottish harp, which harmonises beautifully with her excellent singing voice.

CHICKEN BREAST FILLED WITH SUN-DRIED TOMATO AND FRESH BASIL WRAPPED IN AUBERGINE ON A TOMATO SALSA

2 chicken breasts
6 pieces of sun-dried tomato in oil, drained
6 basil leaves, roughly torn
1 aubergine, preferably a long one
salt and freshly ground black pepper
1 chicken stock cube
olive oil, for shallow-frying

Tomato Salsa:
15 ml (1 tbsp) sun-dried tomato oil
2 shallots, thinly sliced
2 medium ripe tomatoes, skinned, seeded and sliced
4 pieces of sun-dried tomato in oil, drained
250 ml (8 fl oz) passata (sieved tomatoes)
10 ml (2 tsp) red pesto
pinch of caster sugar

To Garnish:
basil leaves

1 Make a deep horizontal slit in the side of each chicken breast to form a pocket. Stuff the pocket with the sun-dried tomato pieces and torn basil leaves. Wrap firmly in greaseproof paper and set aside in a cool place.

2 Cut two lengthwise slices from the aubergine, each about 5 mm (¼ inch) wide and place on a plate. Sprinkle with salt and leave for about 20 minutes to degorge the bitter juces. (Use the rest of the aubergine in another dish.)

3 Bring a medium pan of water to the boil and crumble in the chicken stock cube. Seal the wrapped chicken breasts in boiler bags and add to the boiling stock. Immediately turn the heat down and simmer for approximately 30 minutes.

4 Meanwhile, wash the aubergine slices and pat dry thoroughly. Shallow-fry in olive oil until brown on both sides; the slices should still be soft. Drain well on kitchen paper.

5 For the salsa, heat the sun-dried tomato oil in a pan and fry the shallots for 5 minutes, until just turning brown. Add the fresh tomato slices, the sun-dried tomato pieces and the passata, the pesto and salt, pepper and sugar to taste. Simmer for 12-15 minutes.

6 Lift the chicken out of the stock and unwrap. When cool enough to handle, wrap each piece of chicken in a slice of aubergine, and secure with a cocktail stick. Place on a greased baking tray and brush the chicken and aubergine with 15 ml (1 tbsp) olive oil. Place in a preheated oven at 180°C (350°F) mark 4 for about 7-10 minutes to heat through.

7 To serve, remove the cocktail sticks from the chicken. Ladle some tomato salsa on to each warmed serving plate and position the chicken in the centre. Garnish with basil leaves.

DEGORGING AUBERGINES

Aubergines, especially mature ones, can contain bitter juices. Salting and draining them before cooking helps to remove these juices, and also reduces the aubergine's tendancy to absorb large quantities of oil during cooking. After salting, rinse and dry thoroughly with kitchen paper.

POTATO AND PARSNIP PURÉE

2 large parsnips
1½ medium potatoes
15 ml (1 tbsp) double cream
a little ground cinnamon
small knob of butter
salt and freshly ground white pepper

1 Bring a pan of salted water to the boil. Peel the parsnips and potatoes. Cut the core out of the parsnips and top and tail them. Thinly slice the potato(es). When the water reaches the boil, add the parsnips and turn down the heat. Add the potatoes 4 minutes later and cook both vegetables together until soft enough to push through a sieve.

2 Drain well and immediately press through a sieve into a bowl. Add the cream, cinnamon, butter, salt and pepper; mix thoroughly.

3 Using two tablespoons, form the purée into oval shapes. Place on a greased baking tray. Heat through in a preheated oven at 180°C (350°F) mark 4 until golden brown on top, about 5 minutes. Use a fish slice to transfer them to serving plates.

CRISPY NOODLE NEST FILLED WITH CUCUMBER RIBBONS AND SESAME SEEDS

½ sheet thread egg noodles
1 egg yolk
salt and freshly ground white pepper
a little vegetable oil
15 ml (1 tbsp) sesame seeds
½ long cucumber

1 Bring a pan of water to the boil. Remove from the heat, add the noodles and leave to cook in the residual heat for 3-4 minutes until soft. Drain well, then toss with the egg yolk and seasoning to taste.

2 Grease 2 ramekins with a little oil and line with the egg noodle mixture. Place in a preheated oven at 200°C (400°F) mark 6 for 15-20 minutes. Remove the 'nests' from the ramekins and place upside down on a baking tray. Return to the oven until golden brown all over.

3 Place the sesame seeds on the tray with the 'nests' for 5 minutes, or until golden brown.

4 Using a swivel potato peeler, slice the cucumbers into ribbons. Season with salt and pepper, then pile high in the noodle nests. Sprinkle with the toasted sesame seeds. Serve at once.

APPLE AND LEMON SORBET ON A BLACKCURRANT COULIS

3 Granny Smith apples
juice of ¼ lemon

Sugar Syrup:
150 g (5 oz) caster sugar
300 ml (½ pint) water

Blackcurrant Coulis:
125 g (4 oz) blackcurrants
icing sugar, sifted (optional)

To Decorate:
25 g (1 oz) dark chocolate, broken into pieces
4 mint leaves
1 egg white, lightly beaten
a little caster sugar
a little double cream

1 To make the sugar syrup, put the sugar and water in a saucepan and dissolve over a low heat. Bring to the boil and boil for 3 minutes, then leave to cool completely before use.

2 To make the sorbet, peel, core and slice the apples. Place the apple slices in a heavy-based pan with a little water and simmer for 5 minutes or until soft. Strain through a colander then purée in a food processor or blender. Add the lemon juice and 160 ml (5½ fl oz) of the sugar syrup and blend again until smooth. Place in an electric ice-cream maker and churn for 20 minutes.

3 To make the coulis, hull the blackcurrants and place in a food processor or blender with the remaining sugar syrup. Whizz until the blackcurrants have broken down. Press through a sieve. Taste and add some icing sugar to sweeten if desired. Chill until needed.

4 Melt the chocolate in a heatproof bowl over a pan of hot water. Dip a spoon into the chocolate and drizzle thin 2.5 cm (1 inch) lengths of chocolate on a greaseproof paper lined tray to resemble stalks. These are very fragile, so make more than you need.

5 Dip the mint leaves into beaten egg white, then into caster sugar.

6 Pool the blackcurrant coulis on 2 serving plates. Scoop out 2 balls of sorbet and place one in the middle of each pool of coulis. Dot a little cream onto the coulis and feather with a skewer. Add chocolate stalks and leaves to the 'apple' of sorbet. Serve immediately, accompanied by Hazelnut Heart Biscuits (see overleaf).

COOK'S TIP

If you do not have an electric ice cream maker freeze the mixture in a shallow tray, whisking periodically during freezing to break down the ice crystals and ensure a smooth result.

HAZELNUT HEART BISCUITS

20 g (¾ oz) butter or margarine
7 g (¼ oz) caster sugar
25 g (1 oz) plain flour
20 g (¾ oz) ground hazelnuts

1 Cream the butter and sugar together until light and fluffy, using a mixer or by hand, then mix in the flour a little at a time. Add the ground hazelnuts and mix well to form a smooth dough. Wrap in cling film and place in the refrigerator for 20-30 minutes.

2 Roll the dough out on a lightly floured board until thin, about a 5 mm (¼ inch) thickness. Using a heart-shaped cutter, cut out biscuits. Place carefully on a greased baking tray. Bake in a preheated oven at 180°C (350°F) mark 4 for 7-10 minutes or until crisp and golden brown.

3 Transfer to a wire cooling rack and leave for a couple of minutes before serving warm, with the sorbet.

Makes 5-6 biscuits

REGIONAL HEATS
Scotland

Lindsay Craig's Menu

MAIN COURSE

Roast Pheasant with Chestnuts and Brussels Sprouts

"Exceptionally good pheasant sauce" **Loyd**

Buttered Baby Carrots

Hedgehog Potatoes

DESSERT

Caramelised Rice Pudding with Whisky Marmalade

Twelve year old Lindsay Craig comes from Musselburgh near Edinburgh. At school at the George Watson College Lindsay is happiest working on projects in the new technology block. Like his father, Lindsay is an enthusiastic golfer. He is also a keen competitor on the go-cart track.

ROAST PHEASANT WITH BRUSSELS SPROUTS AND CHESTNUTS

1 large pheasant, plucked and cleaned
2 small thyme sprigs
50 g (2 oz) unsalted butter
30 ml (2 tbsp) walnut oil
salt and freshly ground black pepper

Gravy:
30 ml (2 tbsp) walnut oil
25 g (1 oz) unsalted butter
15 ml (1 tbsp) plain flour
15 ml (1 tbsp) tomato purée
1 onion, diced
1 carrot, diced
1 garlic clove, crushed
3 large thyme sprigs
20 juniper berries

To Garnish:
10 large Brussels sprouts, trimmed
6 baby Brussels sprouts, trimmed
4 chestnuts, shelled and cooked
Hedgehog Potatoes (see right)
Buttered Baby Carrots (see page 28)

1 Place the pheasant on a greased baking tray and, with a knife, cut the skin between body and legs, being careful not to damage the breasts. The legs should fall away limply from the body.

2 Place the thyme on top of the bird and smear with the butter. Pour the walnut oil over. Season lightly and roast in a preheated oven at 190°C (375°F) mark 5 for about 40 minutes. (The timing may vary slightly, depending on your oven type.)

3 The pheasant will be ready when the area of breast visible at the sides is white. Remove from the oven and cut off the legs without damaging the breasts. Skin the legs, and chop meat and bones into fairly small pieces. Keep the rest of the pheasant in a warm place, covered with foil, while you make the gravy.

4 For the gravy, heat the walnut oil and butter together in a pan and gently fry the chopped pheasant legs until brown. Mix the flour, tomato purée and 15 ml (1 tbsp) water to a thick smooth paste and add to the bones. Mix well, making sure that the meat and bones are all covered with paste. Add the onion, carrot, garlic and 600 ml (1 pint) water. Increase the heat and add the thyme and juniper berries. Simmer to reduce until thick enough to coat the back of a spoon. Season to taste and when ready to serve, strain into a gravy boat.

5 Cook the large Brussels sprouts until just tender, and then drain well. Roughly mash – do not purée – and keep warm.

6 Cook the baby sprouts and chestnuts together in a little water for 3-4 minutes only. The sprouts should still be crunchy. Keep warm.

7 To serve, carve the pheasant on the bone and arrange slices in a fan-shape on the warmed serving plates. Using a small round pastry cutter shape a small dome of mashed sprouts on each plate. Place 3 baby sprouts on top of the dome. Garnish with the chestnuts, 2 hedgehog potatoes per plate and the baby carrots. Pour the gravy over the pheasant slices and serve.

HEDGEHOG POTATOES

3 large potatoes
salt
1 packet angel-hair spaghetti (capelli
*   d'angelo)*
50 g (2 oz) unsalted butter
1 egg, beaten
45 ml (3 tbsp) plain flour
sunflower oil for deep-frying

1 Peel the potatoes and cut into even-sized pieces. Cook in lightly salted water until tender, about 20 minutes.

2 Meanwhile, place the spaghetti in a food processor and grind so that the strands are in pieces of about 4-5 mm (¼ inch) long.

3 When the potatoes are cooked, drain well, then mash them with the butter. Form the potato into small balls, using a melon baller or teaspoon and set aside on a tray for a few minutes to dry off.

4 Have ready 3 bowls. In one put the beaten egg, in another put the flour, and in the third put the ground spaghetti. Roll the potato balls first in the flour, then in the egg, and then in the spaghetti.

5 Heat the oil in a deep-fryer. Test to see that it is the correct temperature by dropping a small piece of bread into it: the oil should bubble immediately around the bread. Fry the potato balls in batches in the oil, turning frequently while frying. It will take about 15 seconds for the spaghetti to brown and the balls to be ready. Drain well on kitchen paper. Keep warm.

BUTTERED BABY CARROTS

1 bunch baby carrots
15 ml (1 tbsp) brown sugar
5 ml (1 tsp) ground ginger

1 Top and tail the carrots and put in a pan with the sugar, ginger and enough water to cover.
2 About 15 minutes before the pheasant is ready, cover and cook on a low heat until tender, turning occasionally to glaze. Keep warm.

CARAMELISED RICE PUDDING WITH WHISKY MARMALADE

125 ml (4 fl oz) milk
125 ml (4 fl oz) single cream
⅛ x 397 g (14 oz) can condensed milk
50 g (2 oz) pudding rice
4 heaped teaspoons marmalade
3.75 ml (¾ tsp) whisky
10 ml (2 tsp) brown sugar

1 Put the milk, cream, condensed milk and the rice in a cooking pot or heavy-based pan. Cover and cook slowly until the rice is tender and creamy, about 25 minutes.
2 Flavour the marmalade with the whisky and spread over the bases of two 8 cm (3¼ inch) ramekins.
3 When the rice is cooked, divide it between the ramekins. Sprinkle 5 ml (1 tsp) of brown sugar on each, and put them under a preheated hot grill until the sugar melts and caramelises. Serve immediately.

Contestants
Katie Targett-Adams • Lindsay Craig • Rosemary Morrison

Panel of Judges
Lady Claire Macdonald • Craig Charles • Loyd Grossman

Rosemary Morrison's Menu

MAIN COURSE
Scallop Nests
"Lemon and bacon go perfectly with scallops" **Lady Claire Macdonald**

DESSERT
'Set Sail Strawberries on a Kiwi Sea'

Rosemary Morrison is 10 years of age and comes from Gourock in Renfrewshire. She attends St Columbus' School and is currently in rehearsal for a musical written by the headmaster in which she has been cast wittily as 'The Atrocious Cook'! Rosemary is a keen swimmer and frequently takes to the cool Scottish waters. Her latest pastime is the traditional Scottish sport of curling.

SCALLOP NESTS

225 g (8 oz) fresh Scottish scallops,
   shelled
3 rashers smoked Ayrshire streaky
   bacon, derinded
50 g (2 oz) unsalted butter
5 slices wholemeal bread
1 large egg
30 ml (2 tbsp) milk
olive oil
rock salt
300 g (10 oz) fresh mixed tagliatelle
   (plain, tomato and spinach)

Lemon Sauce:
150 ml (¼ pint) white wine vinegar
15 ml (1 tbsp) granulated sugar
juice of 2 large lemons
5 ml (1 tsp) cornflour, mixed with 5 ml
   (1 tsp) water
5 ml (1 tsp) unsalted butter

1 Snip the bacon rashers into small pieces using kitchen scissors (not too small as they will shrink on cooking). Toss in a small frying pan over moderate heat with a little of the butter until crisp. Drain and keep warm.

2 Cut the crusts off the bread, and make the bread into crumbs, using a grater, food processor or blender. Beat the egg and milk together in a bowl.

3 Dip the scallops in the egg and milk mixture, then in the breadcrumbs to coat well. Keep to one side.

4 Bring a large pan of water to the boil, then add 4 drops of olive oil and a pinch of rock salt. Immerse the fresh tagliatelle in the water, stir and cook for about 7-8 minutes until *al dente* (tender but firm to the bite). Bring a kettle of water to the boil to rinse the tagliatelle after boiling.

4 Heat the rest of the butter and 30 ml (2 tbsp) of olive oil in a large frying pan. When hot, pan-fry the bread-crumbed scallops for 2-3 minutes on each side, depending on the thickness of the scallops. Drain and keep warm.

5 Meanwhile, make the sauce. Stir the vinegar and sugar in a small pan over gentle heat until the sugar has dissolved. Bring to the boil and boil rapidly, without stirring, until the mixture turns a light golden brown. Add the strained lemon juice, bring to the boil again, then reduce the heat. Let the mixture simmer until reduced by half. Add the cornflour and stir constantly over the heat until the sauce boils and thickens. Add the butter just before serving.

6 Drain the tagliatelle well, and rinse with the boiling water. Drain and shake dry.

7 Place the tagliatelle on warmed serving plates, leaving a space in the middle for the scallops. Scatter the snippets of bacon over the tagliatelle, and serve the lemon sauce in a small jug to pour over.

TO PREPARE SCALLOPS
Scrub the shells thoroughly under cold running water. Holding the scallop shell level in your palm, flat shell upwards, insert a strong knife between the shells and twist to open. Sever the muscle and loosen the meat from the shell. Discard the dark muscle and beard-like fringe.

'SET SAIL STRAWBERRIES ON A KIWI SEA'

Granita:
10 ml (2 tsp) brandy
60 ml (4 tbsp) water
65 g (2½ oz) caster sugar
250 g (9 oz) fresh strawberries, hulled
150 g (5 oz) low-fat natural yogurt
1 large egg white, stiffly beaten

Oatmeal Boat Barquettes:
65 g (2½ oz) unsalted butter
30 g (1¼ oz) demerara sugar
7.5 ml (½ tbsp) golden syrup
125 g (4 oz) oatmeal or porridge oats

To Decorate:
4 firm but ripe kiwi fruit, skinned and
*   sliced*

1 For the granitas, the night before, combine the brandy, water and sugar in a saucepan, and stir constantly over a gentle heat without letting it boil until the sugar has dissolved. Bring to the boil, then reduce the heat and simmer, uncovered and without stirring, for about 3 minutes or until the mixture is thick. Cool the sugar syrup to room temperature.

2 Set aside 4 good-sized strawberries for the sails. Put the bulk of the strawberries into the blender with the yogurt, and blend until smooth. Add the cooled sugar syrup, and blend again until combined. Pour the mixture into a small shallow freezing container and cover with foil. Freeze for 4-5 hours until set. This time is required for the flavours to fully develop.

3 Break up the mixture, using a fork, and fold in the beaten egg white. Put the mixture back into the freezer, covered, for about 1 hour or until firm.

4 Meanwhile, make the barquettes. Grease 6 small boat-shaped tartlet tins, each about 10 cm (4 inches) long, with 5 ml (1 tsp) of the butter.

5 Melt the rest of the butter, the sugar and the syrup together in a saucepan over a very low heat, stirring with a wooden spoon. Take the pan off the heat, add the oatmeal or porridge oats and mix well. Set aside until cool enough to handle.

6 Divide the mixture into six. Put one piece in each boat tin, and flatten and smooth out using your fingers. Make sure the mixture reaches the edges and has a neat finish. Fill with foil or grease-proof paper and baking beans. Place on a baking sheet. Bake blind in a preheated oven at 180°C (350°F) mark 4 for about 10 minutes, or until golden brown. Leave in the tins for 2 minutes, then turn the boats carefully out on to a wire cooling rack and leave until cold.

7 To serve, arrange the barquettes on chilled plates. Surround with kiwi slices - these form the sea! Spoon the strawberry granita into the boats, using teaspoons. Slice the reserved strawberries from the point down. Make 3 dents in each portion of granita using a knife, and place the strawberry slices upwards into the granita to form the sails. Serve immediately.

REGIONAL HEATS
—— The South West & Wales ——

Contestants
Gaia Skibinski • Reece Dominy • Erika Powell

Panel of Judges
Paul Rankin • Paula Hamilton • Loyd Grossman

WINNER

Gaia Skibinski's Menu

MAIN COURSE
Risotto with Herbs and Prawns

DESSERT
Zabaglione Ice Cream
"Very creamy and delicious" **Paula Hamilton**

Gaia Skibinski comes from Swansea in South Wales and is 14 years old. Gaia attends Olchfa School where she's a stalwart member of the cross country team. She is currently completing her Duke of Edinburgh Bronze medal, and is doing her community service at the local fire station. Gaia's mother is a keen cook too, and appeared in MasterChef a few years ago.

RISOTTO WITH HERBS AND PRAWNS

300 g (10 oz) large raw prawns in shell
7.5 ml (½ tbsp) olive oil
½ onion, finely chopped
250 g (9 oz) arborio rice
½ wine glass dry white wine
salt and freshly ground white pepper
15 ml (1 tbsp) chopped herbs (parsley,
  chervil, tarragon, chives)
30 g (1¼ oz) butter

Fish Stock:
1 onion
1 carrot
1 leek
fish bones, preferably from sole
bouquet garni (celery stick, parsley
  stalks, bay leaf, thyme sprigs)
white peppercorns

1 Make the fish stock first. Cut the vegetables and fish bones into small pieces. Put all the ingredients together in a large pan with enough water to cover – at least 1 litre (1¾ pints). Bring to the boil, turn down to simmer and skim off any scum. Simmer for 20 minutes. Strain through a muslin-lined sieve. (The stock can be strengthened by further boiling and reducing if desired.) Add salt if necessary.

2 Peel the prawns, leaving on the tail shells if preferred, and remove the black intestinal vein.

3 To prepare the risotto, heat the oil in a heavy-based saucepan and sauté the onion until transparent. Add the rice and stir to coat in the oil. Add the wine and cook until it is absorbed.

4 Add a ladleful of stock and stir until absorbed. Continue to add the stock in ladlefuls, until the rice is cooked. This will take about 20 minutes; the rice should be tender but still firm to the bite. Season with salt and pepper to taste.

5 Remove the saucepan from the heat and stir in the herbs and a little of the butter.

6 Meanwhile, melt the remaining butter in a pan, add the prawns and cook them very briefly until they turn pink. Serve the risotto on warmed individual plates, shaped in a ring if you like, with the prawns arranged decoratively on top.

ARBORIO RICE

Arborio rice is the classic Italian risotto rice. It has the capacity to absorb plenty of liquid on cooking without turning soft and starchy.

ZABAGLIONE ICE CREAM

2 eggs, separated
30 ml (2 tbsp) caster sugar
30 ml (2 tbsp) amaretto di Saronno
* liqueur*
125 ml (4 fl oz) double or whipping
* cream*
3 amaretti biscuits, crushed

To Decorate:
seasonal fruit
icing sugar, for dusting

1 Put the egg yolks into a bowl with the sugar and liqueur. Stand the bowl in a pan filled with warm water. Whisk constantly at an even rhythm for about 10 minutes over gentle heat until the mixture is light, foamy and pale yellow.

2 Take the bowl off the heat, put over a pan of cold water and continue to whisk until the mixture has cooled down.

3 Whip the cream and the egg whites together. Fold this mixture carefully into the egg yolks.

4 Add the crushed amaretti biscuits and pour the mixture into an ice-cream maker. Churn for about 20 minutes to freeze.

5 When the ice cream is ready, place two scoops on each chilled serving plate. Decorate with fruit and dust with icing sugar. Serve immediately.

COOK'S TIP

If you do not have an ice cream maker, freeze the ice cream in a shallow container, whisking periodically during freezing to break down the ice crystals and ensure a smooth result.

Contestants
Gaia Skibinski • Reece Dominy • Erika Powell

Panel of Judges
Paul Rankin • Paula Hamilton • Loyd Grossman

Reece Dominy's Menu

MAIN COURSE
Turkey Marsala
"Marsala Sauce with turkey – a lovely balance" **Paul Rankin**
Baby New Potatoes
Buttered Carrots
Mangetouts

DESSERT
Lemon Sabayon

Eleven year old Reece Dominy lives in Amesbury in Wiltshire. Reece's family have recently returned from America where his father was a chef in the US Air Force. Reece now goes to the Bishop Wordsworth School next to Salisbury Cathedral. One of his favourite leisure pursuits is ten-pin bowling. He is also a keen model maker.

TURKEY MARSALA

*1-2 turkey breasts, about 175 g (6 oz)
  each
30 ml (2 tbsp) plain flour
pinch of mace
pinch of paprika
pinch of dried basil
pinch of dried oregano
salt and freshly ground black pepper
30 ml (2 tbsp) oil
25 g (1 oz) butter
150 ml (¼ pint) Marsala wine
150 ml (¼ pint) double cream
juice of ½ lemon
50 g (2 oz) button mushrooms, thinly
  sliced*

To Garnish:
5 ml (1 tsp) chopped parsley

1 Place the turkey breasts on a chopping board and beat each one with a meat mallet, to flatten as much as possible.

2 Sift the flour on to a plate and mix in the mace, paprika, basil, oregano, salt and pepper.

3 Coat each turkey breast in the seasoned flour and shake off any excess. Heat the oil and butter in a large frying pan. When it is sizzling hot, add the turkey breasts and fry for 2 minutes on each side or until cooked and golden brown.

4 Pour the Marsala into the pan and allow to boil for 2 minutes. Stir in the cream and lemon juice, and boil for 1 minute, shaking the pan constantly.

5 Transfer the chicken breasts to warmed serving plates using a fish slice or spatula. Add the mushrooms to the sauce left in the pan. Simmer, stirring continuously, for 2 minutes, then pour over the chicken. Serve at once, garnished with a little chopped parsley.

LEMON SABAYON

2 egg yolks
½ whole egg (size 2)
25 g (1 oz) caster sugar
finely grated rind and juice of ½ lemon
7.5 ml (½ tbsp) Cointreau
90 ml (3 fl oz) sweet vermouth

1 Place the egg yolks, egg and sugar together in a bowl and whisk for 5 minutes.

2 Whisk in the lemon rind and juice, Cointreau and vermouth.

3 Place the bowl over a pan of hot water and continue to whisk over gentle heat until the mixture is thick and pale.

4 Remove the bowl from the heat and whisk, over a pan of cold water if you like, until the mixture is cool. Spoon into individual dishes and serve chilled.

REGIONAL HEATS
— The South West & Wales —

Contestants
Gaia Skibinski • Reece Dominy • Erika Powell

Panel of Judges
Paul Rankin • Paula Hamilton • Loyd Grossman

Erika Powell's Menu

MAIN COURSE
Hot and Spicy Chicken Livers
Glazed Onions
Seasonal Vegetables

DESSERT
Walnut and Orange Stars, with Butterscotch Sauce
"Really yummy!" **Paula Hamilton**

Erika Powell comes from Burnham-on-Sea in Somerset and is 15 years old. A pupil at King Alfred's School, Erika enjoys a wide variety of sports, from gymnastics to ladies football. Erika is also a member of the St John's Ambulance Brigade and is well practised in many of the essential life saving techniques.

HOT AND SPICY CHICKEN LIVERS

225 g (8 oz) chicken livers
plain flour, for coating
60 ml (4 tbsp) olive oil
5 ml (1 tsp) coarsely ground black
  pepper
10 ml (2 tsp) chopped coriander
1 garlic clove, crushed
150 ml (¼ pint) chicken stock
15 ml (1 tbsp) natural yogurt

To Garnish:
coriander leaves

1 Trim the chicken livers, rinse and pat dry, then cut into small pieces. Toss in flour to coat evenly.

2 Mix the oil with the black pepper, coriander and garlic in a dish. Heat up a frying pan gently.

3 Pour the oil mixture into the heated frying pan and, when hot, add the chicken livers. Fry, stirring, until sealed on all sides, then add the chicken stock. Simmer gently until cooked, approximately 10 minutes.

4 When cooked, remove the livers from the pan and keep warm. Add the yogurt to the pan juices and stir over a low heat to make a sauce. Pour the sauce over the livers and garnish with coriander. Serve with the glazed onions and vegetables of your choice.

GLAZED ONIONS

225 g (8 oz) pickling onions, peeled
25 g (1 oz) butter
150 ml (¼ pint) chicken stock
15 ml (1 tbsp) caster sugar

1 Melt the butter in a frying pan, add the onions and sauté until lightly browned.

2 Stir in the stock and sugar. Bring to the boil, then turn down heat and simmer for 15-20 minutes or until the stock has reduced to a syrup and caramelised. Serve hot.

COOK'S TIP

The easiest way to peel pickling onions is to place them in a pan of water, bring to the boil and simmer for 30 seconds to loosen the skins. Drain and refresh under cold water. You should then be able to slip the onions out of their skins easily.

WALNUT AND ORANGE STARS WITH BUTTERSCOTCH SAUCE

Stars:
3 eggs, separated
125 g (4 oz) caster sugar
grated rind of 1 orange
45 ml (3 tbsp) orange juice
50 g (2 oz) walnuts, finely chopped
125 g (4 oz) self-raising flour
icing sugar, for dredging

Butterscotch Sauce:
25 g (1 oz) butter
50 g (2 oz) dark muscovado sugar
5 ml (1 tsp) plain flour
120 ml (4 fl oz) milk

To Decorate:
orange segments and lemon balm or
*   mint leaves*

1 Preheat the oven to 200°C (400°F) mark 6. Grease and line a 33 x 23 cm (13 x 9 inch) Swiss roll tin. Whisk the egg yolks and sugar together in a bowl until pale, then gently fold in the orange rind and juice with the walnuts.

2 Sift the flour over the mixture and fold in, using a metal spoon. Whisk the egg whites until stiff and fold into the egg mixture. Pour into the tin evenly. Bake for 12-15 minutes until risen and golden. Turn out, peel off the lining paper and leave to cool on a wire rack.

3 To make the sauce, melt the butter in a pan, add the sugar and stir over a low heat until dissolved; remove from the heat. Blend the flour with a little of the milk to make a smooth paste, then stir in the remaining milk. Stir the milk mixture into the butter mixture and return the pan to the heat. Simmer, stirring constantly, until slightly thickened and smooth; cool slightly.

4 Using a 10 cm (4 inch) star cutter, cut four stars from the Swiss roll and liberally sift icing sugar over them. Arrange on dessert plates and pour the sauce around them. Decorate with orange segments and lemon balm or mint leaves.

Note: This recipe serves 4.

London

Contestants
Yoav Preiss • Francesca Alberry • Amber Arnold

Panel of Judges
Eugene McCoy • Chris Packham • Loyd Grossman

WINNER

Yoav Preiss' Menu

MAIN COURSE
Spiced Stuffed Poussin on a Red Pepper Coulis
Vegetable Soufflés
Aubergine Slices in a Piquant Dressing
"Seriously good marinade on the aubergine" **Eugene McCoy**

DESSERT
Summer Fruit Cup with a Raspberry Sorbet and Cream

From North Finchley, Yoav Preiss is twelve years of age. Much of Yoav's spare time is currently spent in the synagogue preparing for his Barmitzvah. He is also a keen tennis player and his game is improving all the time.

SPICED STUFFED POUSSIN ON A RED PEPPER COULIS

1 poussin
2.5 ml (½ tsp) paprika
2.5 ml (½ tsp) zahtar
freshly ground black pepper
1 garlic clove, crushed
½ onion, chopped
45 ml (3 tbsp) olive oil

Stuffing:
15 ml (1 tbsp) vegetable oil
1 medium onion, chopped
2 garlic cloves, crushed
1.25 ml (¼ tsp) ground coriander
1.25 ml (¼ tsp) ground cumin
1.25 ml (¼ tsp) turmeric
1.25 ml (¼ tsp) zahtar
350 g (12 oz) lean minced beef
2 slices day-old white bread, diced
15 ml (1 tbsp) chopped parsley
1 egg

Red Pepper Coulis:
3 red peppers
7.5 ml (½ tbsp) chopped parsley
3 basil leaves
5 ml (1 tsp) olive oil
1.25 ml (¼ tsp) salt
1.25 ml (¼ tsp) freshly ground black
   pepper

To Garnish:
lamb's lettuce

1 To make the stuffing, heat the oil in a pan and fry the onion and garlic gently until golden brown.

2 Add the spices to the beef mince, along with the onion and garlic, bread and parsley. Mix briefly, then add the egg and mix well to bind the stuffing.

3 Stuff this into the poussin and secure the opening with wooden cocktail sticks.

4 Place the poussin on a baking tray and sprinkle with the spices, garlic and onion. Pour over the oil and bake in a preheated oven at 160°C (325°F) mark 3 for 40-45 minutes until tender.

5 Meanwhile make the red pepper coulis. Char the whole peppers under a hot grill until black all over. Place in a closed container to allow them to sweat, and leave for 10 minutes. Remove the skins under cold water, then halve the peppers and remove the seeds.

6 Put the skinless peppers and remaining coulis ingredients into a blender or food processor and work to a pureé. Leave to one side.

7 When the poussin is cooked, transfer to a warmed serving dish and leave to rest for a few moments, before cutting into slices. Pour the juices from the baking tray into the coulis, and stir to mix.

8 Serve the poussin slices on warmed serving plates, with the coulis. Serve the vegetable soufflé and sliced aubergine accompaniments on a side plate.

ZAHTAR

Zahtar is a Middle Eastern spice mixture, comprising sumac, toasted sesame seeds and powdered dried thyme. It is available from delicatessens.

VEGETABLE SOUFFLÉS

5 ml (1 tsp) vegetable oil
1 small onion, finely chopped
2 medium potatoes, peeled and
    quartered
25 g (1 oz) vegetable(s) of choice
    (peas, chopped carrot, celery etc)
1 egg, separated
pinch each of ground cumin, coriander,
    paprika
salt and freshly ground black pepper
2.5 ml (½ tsp) baking powder

1 Heat the oil in a frying pan and gently fry the onion until soft. Meanwhile, separately cook the potatoes and other vegetables in boiling salted water until tender. Drain well.

2 Skin and mash the potatoes, then add the fried onion, egg yolk, vegetables, spices, seasoning and baking powder.

3 Beat the egg white until stiff, and carefully fold into the mashed potato mixture.

4 Oil 2 ramekins well and divide the soufflé mixture between them. Cook in a preheated oven at 180°C (350°F) mark 4 for 10-15 minutes, until well risen and golden.

5 Turn the soufflés out of the ramekins and serve immediately.

SLICED AUBERGINE IN A PIQUANT DRESSING

1 medium aubergine
a little oil, for frying

Dressing:
juice of 1 lemon
15 ml (1 tbsp) olive oil
2.5 ml (½ tsp) soy sauce
2.5 ml (½ tsp) Worcestershire sauce
1 garlic clove, crushed
salt and freshly ground black pepper
pinch each of dry mustard, ground
    cumin and paprika
chopped coriander, to taste

1 Slice the aubergine into rounds, about 1 cm (½ inch) thick.

2 Heat a griddle or heavy-based frying pan and wipe with a little oil. Fry the aubergine slices on both sides until cooked and golden.

3 Meanwhile, make the dressing. Put all of the ingredients in a screw-topped jar and shake vigorously to combine.

4 Arrange the aubergine slices on warmed side plates, spoon over the dressing and serve immediately.

SUMMER FRUIT CUP WITH A RASPBERRY SORBET AND CREAM

225 g (8 oz) soft summer fruits
(strawberries, raspberries,
redcurrants, etc)
45 ml (3 tbsp) cherry liqueur or kirsch
7.5 ml (½ tbsp) icing sugar

Sorbet:
225 g (8 oz) fresh raspberries
30 ml (2 tbsp) cherry liqueur or kirsch
15 ml (1 tbsp) icing sugar
1 egg white

To Serve:
50 ml (2 fl oz) double or whipping
cream

1 First make the sorbet. Purée the raspberries in a blender or food processor with the liqueur and icing sugar.

2 Whisk the egg white until firm, then fold into the raspberry mixture. Pour into a shallow container and freeze until firm, whisking periodically during freezing to break down the ice crystals. Alternatively churn in an ice-cream maker until firm.

3 Prepare the summer fruit as appropriate, then macerate in the liqueur with the icing sugar.

4 Just before serving, heat the summer fruit through briefly. Whip the cream until thick.

5 Spoon the hot summer fruits into the bottom of 2 Irish coffee glasses. Liquidise the cold sorbet and pour over the fruit. Top with the whipped cream. Serve immediately.

Contestants
Yoav Preiss • Francesca Alberry • Amber Arnold

Panel of Judges
Eugene McCoy • Chris Packham • Loyd Grossman

Francesca Alberry's Menu

MAIN COURSE
Pork Fillet in Ginger Wine
New Potatoes
Cauliflower and Broccoli

DESSERT
Poached Apricots with Amaretto Cream
"Mmmm... it's good!" **Loyd**

Twelve year old Francesca Alberry comes from East Sheen. She is a talented artist and, during school holidays, takes part in courses run by painter Pauline Jones from her home in St Leonard's, East Sussex. Francesca is also learning to play the guitar.

PORK FILLET IN GINGER WINE

1 pork fillet
seasoned flour, for coating
25 g (1 oz) butter
15 ml (1 tbsp) olive oil
90 ml (3 fl oz) ginger wine
15 ml (1 tbsp) lemon juice
45 ml (3 tbsp) crème fraîche
salt and freshly ground black pepper

To Garnish:
few slices of pickled Japanese ginger

1 First cut the pork fillet into slices, approximately 2.5 cm (1 inch) thick. Place between cling film and beat out flat with a rolling pin.

2 Dip the flattened pork slices in seasoned flour. Heat the butter and olive oil in a frying pan, add the pork slices and fry, turning occasionally, for about 6 minutes or until browned and cooked through. Place in a warmed dish in a low oven to keep hot.

3 Add the ginger wine to the frying pan, stirring to scrape up the sediment. Simmer gently for 5 minutes until it has become syrupy. Stir in the lemon juice and crème fraîche and simmer for 3 minutes. Add 2 twists of pepper and a pinch of salt.

4 Serve immediately, garnished with the Japanese ginger.

POACHED APRICOTS WITH AMARETTO CREAM

75 g (3 oz) caster sugar
juice of ½ lemon
1 vanilla pod, split
2 apricots
2 lemon slices
few drops of amaretto di Saronno
*   liqueur, or to taste*
60 ml (4 tbsp) single cream
2 amaretti biscuits, crushed

1 Place 50 g (2 oz) of the sugar in a pan with the lemon juice, vanilla pod and 450 ml (¾ pint) water. Stir over a low heat until the sugar dissolves. Bring to the boil, reduce to a simmer, then add the apricots and simmer for about 5 minutes.

2 Remove the apricots from the syrup with a slotted spoon; leave to cool slightly, then peel. Meanwhile, boil the syrup rapidly for 10 minutes until well reduced; strain and leave to cool.

3 Put the remaining sugar and 30 ml (2 tbsp) water in a small heavy-based pan and dissolve over a low heat. Increase the heat and boil rapidly until it turns a golden caramel colour.

4 Add the lemon slices to the syrup carefully as the mixture is very hot and may spit. Stir with a wooden spoon to coat in the caramel; leave to cool slightly.

5 Add a few drops of amaretto to the cream. Place a lemon slice on each serving plate, set an apricot on top and pour over a little of the syrup. Sprinkle over the crushed amaretti and drizzle over the amaretto cream.

AMARETTO

Amaretto di Saronno is an Italian liqueur, flavoured with apricot kernels, which has a distinctive almond-like flavour. If unobtainable, you could flavour the cream with a dash of Grand Marnier instead.

Contestants

Yoav Preiss • Francesca Alberry • Amber Arnold

Panel of Judges

Eugene McCoy • Chris Packham • Loyd Grossman

Amber Arnold's Menu

MAIN COURSE

Salmon in Puff Pastry with Dill Sauce

"Well balanced dill sauce" **Eugene McCoy**

Potatoes

Mangetouts

DESSERT

Poached Red Pears with Toasted Almonds

Amber Arnold from Notting Hill is 15 years old. Amber attends Campden School for Girls where she is an active member of the council which meets regularly to sort out the school's problems. She particularly enjoys the arts subjects and recently made ornate Art Nouveau tiles for a pottery project. At home no corner of the house is safe from her imaginative stencil brush!

SALMON IN PUFF PASTRY WITH DILL SAUCE

2 salmon cutlets, boned and cut into
  chunks
salt and freshly ground white pepper
2 dill sprigs
15 g (½ oz) butter

Pastry:
225 g (8 oz) plain flour
150 g (5 oz) butter
60 ml (4 tbsp) water (approximately)

Dill Sauce:
few dill sprigs
45 ml (3 tbsp) white wine vinegar
60 ml (4 tbsp) water
1 shallot, finely chopped
225 g (8 oz) chilled butter, diced

1 For the pastry, sift the flour and 5 ml (1 tsp) salt into a bowl. Rub in 50 g (2 oz) of the butter until the mixture resembles breadcrumbs. Mix in enough water to obtain a fairly dry dough.

2 Roll out the dough thinly on a lightly floured surface to a rectangle, then dot about a third of the rest of the butter on top. Fold the dough in half over the butter, and roll out in one direction until thin again. Do this twice more to use up all the butter. (Add more flour if it seems too moist.) Wrap the pastry in cling film and chill in the refrigerator for 10 minutes.

3 Roll the pastry out to about a 3 mm (⅛ inch) thickness and cut out 2 simple fish shapes, each 15 cm (6 inches) long. Place chunks of salmon on top and season with salt and pepper. Top with a dill sprig. Dot with butter. Cut 2 appropriately sized squares from the remaining pastry and place over the fish. Push down the edges over the salmon to meet the edge of the pastry fish shape. Moisten with water and press together firmly. Shape, cutting away excess pastry. You should have 2 rounded fish shapes. Make sure the pastry is well sealed. Decorate with fins and scales, using the tip of a spoon or scissors. Chill for 10 minutes.

4 Cook in a preheated oven at 220°C (425°F) mark 7 for 20-30 minutes.

5 Meanwhile make the dill sauce. Separate the dill leaves from the stems; finely chop the stems. Put the vinegar, water and shallot together in a saucepan and bring to the boil, then boil steadily to reduce to a glaze. Strain out the shallot. Add the butter, a piece at a time, whisking constantly over a high heat. Bring the sauce to the boil. Add the chopped dill stems and whisk for a further minute. Before serving, add the dill leaves.

6 Place a salmon puff on each warmed serving plate and serve with the dill sauce.

POACHED RED PEARS WITH TOASTED ALMONDS

2 red pears
40 g (1½ oz) flaked almonds
150 g (5 oz) caster sugar
150 ml (¼ pint) red wine
2.5 cm (1 inch) piece of cinnamon stick
10 ml (2 tsp) arrowroot

To Serve:
a little whipped cream (optional)

1 Toast the almonds on a baking tray in a preheated oven at 180°C (350°F) mark 4 for about 10 minutes, shaking twice, until golden brown. Allow to cool.

2 Put the sugar, wine and 150 ml (¼ pint) water in a heavy-based saucepan with the cinnamon stick. Place over a low heat until the sugar has dissolved then boil steadily for 5 minutes.

3 Peel the pears and cut a thin slice off the bottom of each one with a sharp knife, to enable them to stand well. Leave on the stalks. Place the pears in the syrup and simmer for 20-30 minutes or until translucent and soft. Take out the pears and arrange on individual plates.

4 Discard the cinnamon stick from the syrup. Mix the arrowroot with 15 ml (1 tbsp) water, then add to the syrup. Bring to the boil and simmer, stirring, for 1 minute until clear. Spoon over the pears and sprinkle with almonds. Serve warm, with whipped cream, if desired.

COOKING PEARS

Choose small, firm red-skinned pears which 'give' a little at the stem end. Different varieties are available all year round. Look out for Red Williams and Red Bartlett pears.

Contestants
Katy Savage • Rebecca Beal • Katherine Smith

Panel of Judges
Nick Nairn • Anneka Rice • Loyd Grossman

WINNER

Katy Savage's Menu

MAIN COURSE
Poached Halibut in a Light Tarragon Mustard Sauce
"Lovely light sauce" **Anneka Rice**
Bean Bundles
Timbale of Three Kinds of Rice

DESSERT
Harvest Fruits Amandine

Katy Savage is thirteen and lives in Newcastle upon Tyne. Katy is a leading light in the music group of The Sacred Heart School and often plays the piano at school assembly. She is also keen on tennis and gives her father a good run for his money! An Archers' addict, Katie always makes sure she's home in time for her daily dose of Ambridge life.

POACHED HALIBUT IN A LIGHT TARRAGON MUSTARD SAUCE

2 halibut steaks
salt and freshly ground black pepper

Court Bouillon:
2 shallots, finely chopped
1 carrot, finely chopped
1 celery stick, finely chopped
1 bay leaf
1 bouquet garni
200 ml (7 fl oz) dry white wine
scant 600 ml (1 pint) water

Sauce:
reserved court bouillon (see method)
5 ml (1 tsp) tarragon mustard
45 ml (3 tbsp) crème fraîche

1 To make the court bouillon, put all the ingredients into a pan and season with salt and pepper. Bring to the boil, lower the heat and simmer for 20 minutes. Strain the court bouillon into the pan you will use for poaching the halibut. Discard the vegetables.

2 Pat the halibut steaks dry with kitchen paper. Bring the court bouillon to the boil, then put the halibut steaks in the pan. Reduce the heat, cover and poach for 8 minutes or until the halibut is cooked. Carefully remove the fish from the liquid, using a fish slice, and place in a warmed dish. Cover and keep warm in a low oven. Strain and reserve about 150 ml (¼ pint) liquid.

3 For the sauce, pour the reserved court bouillon into a small pan and boil rapidly until reduced by about a third. Turn the heat down and add the tarragon mustard and crème fraîche. Season with salt and pepper to taste and stir well.

4 Pool the sauce on 2 warmed serving plates and place the fish on top, with the accompanying bean bundles and rice timbales. Serve at once.

HALIBUT

Halibut is the largest of the flat sea fish and is regarded as one of the finest flavoured of all fish. It is available all year round but is at its best from June to March.

BEAN BUNDLES

24 fine green beans
salt and freshly ground black pepper
knob of butter
2 rashers of streaky bacon
10 ml (2 tsp) olive oil
50 ml (2 fl oz) red wine vinegar

1 Top and tail the beans, then put into a pan with enough salted water to cover. Cook over a moderate heat for about 15 minutes. Drain and return them to the pan. Add the butter and season with salt and pepper.

2 Stretch the bacon rashers, using the back of a fork. Place in a frying pan without additional fat and fry for a few minutes until not quite done (because you will be frying them again later).

3 Lay 12 beans on each piece of bacon, and make a hole in one end of the bacon. Pass the opposite end of the bacon through the hole, and pull tight around the beans.

4 Add the oil and vinegar to the bacon frying pan, then add the bean bundles and cook for a couple of minutes. Serve immediately or keep warm on a baking tray in a low oven until required.

TIMBALE OF THREE KINDS OF RICE

150 g (5 oz) mixed rice (long-grain white, wild and brown)
salt and freshly ground black pepper
10 ml (2 tsp) olive oil
knob of butter
1 onion, finely chopped

1 Bring 1.2 litres (2 pints) salted water to the boil in a pan. Wash the rice, drain and add to the boiling salted water. Cover and cook over a moderate heat for 20 minutes, then drain. Return the rice to the pan and season very well with salt and pepper.

2 While the rice is cooking, heat the oil and butter together in a small frying pan and cook the onion until translucent. Add to the rice and mix well.

3 Line 2 ramekins with foil and pack the rice in very tightly. (I always end up with too much rice, so don't worry if there's slightly more than you need.) Cover the ramekins with foil to stop the rice becoming too dry, and keep warm in a low oven.

4 To turn out, remove the foil and invert a ramekin on to each warmed serving plate. Remove the ramekins and foil. Serve at once.

HARVEST FRUITS AMANDINE

250 g (9 oz) ground almonds
250 g (9 oz) caster sugar
3 eggs
90 ml (3 fl oz) milk
3 drops of vanilla essence
30 ml (2 tbsp) pine nuts
75 ml (5 tbsp) blackberry jelly

Pear Coulis:
4 pears
½ lemon
5 ml (1 tsp) granulated sugar

To Decorate:
2 blackberries
4-6 mint leaves

1 Preheat the oven to 180°C (350°F) mark 4 and line a 23 cm (9 inch) round cake tin with buttered foil.

2 To make the amandine, mix the ground almonds and sugar together in a bowl. Beat in the eggs, milk and vanilla essence until smooth. Pour into the prepared cake tin and sprinkle the top with the pine nuts. Bake in the oven for 45 minutes or until the top is brown and the cake feels firm to the touch. Turn out and cool on a wire rack.

3 Put the blackberry jelly into a saucepan and heat gently until it has melted. If it is not melting very well, add a little water. Pour over the amandine and spread it evenly with a knife. Leave to one side.

4 To make the pear coulis, finely pare 2 strips of rind from the lemon half and put into a small saucepan. Squeeze in the lemon juice.

5 Peel, core and slice the pears thinly. Add to the saucepan and turn in the lemon juice to stop them discolouring. Add the sugar and a little water. Cover and simmer until the pears have become translucent. Remove the lid and continue simmering to evaporate some of the juices. Discard the lemon rind. Force the pears through a sieve with the flat edge of a wooden spoon into a bowl to make a smooth coulis. Allow to cool.

6 Serve the amandine and the pear coulis when they are cold. Pour the coulis around each plate and serve a wedge of amandine on top. Decorate with a blackberry and a few mint leaves.

Contestants
Katy Savage • Rebecca Beal • Katherine Smith

Panel of Judges
Nick Nairn • Anneka Rice • Loyd Grossman

Rebecca Beal's Menu

MAIN COURSE
Calves Liver in a Cassis Sauce, with Caramelised Fruit
and Vegetables

Warm Mushroom and Bacon Salad

New Potato Gâteau

DESSERT
Bread and Butter Pudding with a Caramel Sauce
and Ginger Anglaise

"Wonderful pudding... particularly the caramelised sauce" **Anneka Rice**

From Whitley Bay, Rebecca Beal is 13 years old. Rebecca goes to Marden Bridge Middle School where she is a stalwart of the netball team. After school she loves to further her energetic pursuits with her friends at the nearby 'Wet & Wild' water sports park. At home Rebecca turns her hand to intricate crafts, including making impressive dolls houses with her mother.

CALVES LIVER IN A CASSIS SAUCE, WITH CARAMELISED FRUIT AND VEGETABLES

225 g (8 oz) calves liver, thinly sliced
25 g (1 oz) seasoned flour
olive oil for frying
15 g (½ oz) butter
¼ small onion, finely chopped
1 garlic clove, crushed
1 rosemary sprig
50 g (2 oz) blackcurrants
25 ml (1 fl oz) blackcurrant vinegar
50 ml (2 fl oz) chicken stock
50 ml (2 fl oz) crème de cassis
salt and freshly ground black pepper

Caramelised Fruit and Vegetables:
50 g (2 oz) fresh pineapple
¼ red pepper, seeded
¼ chilli, seeded
1 bunch spring onions
15 g (½ oz) butter
20 ml (4 tsp) caster sugar

1 Dip the liver in seasoned flour to coat, shaking off excess. Heat a little olive oil and the butter in a frying pan, add the liver slices and sauté lightly and quickly until tender. Remove from the pan with a slotted spoon and keep warm.

2 Add the onion and garlic to the pan, and cook quickly, avoiding colouring the onion, until soft.

3 Add the rosemary, blackcurrants and vinegar to the pan, and cook on a high heat for 1 minute, allowing the juices to reduce.

4 Add the stock and cassis, and reduce until the sauce thickens slightly: it is very important that the sauce is not reduced too much. Adjust the seasoning and strain. Keep to one side.

5 Slice the pineapple, pepper and chilli finely. Cut the spring onions into 2.5 cm (1 inch) pieces.

6 Melt the butter in a heavy-based pan, and add the pineapple, pepper, chilli and spring onions. Cook quickly for 1 minute, then add the sugar and cook fast to caramelise. Keep to one side.

7 To serve, reheat the liver quickly under a hot grill if necessary. Heat the sauce through. Arrange the caramelised fruit and vegetables on one side of each warmed plate and fan the liver out on top. Serve with the New Potato Gâteau and Mushroom and Bacon Salad.

NEW POTATO GATEAU

4 medium new potatoes, washed
25 g (1 oz) butter
50 g (2 oz) leek (white part only), thinly
    sliced
½ small onion, thinly sliced
25 ml (1 fl oz) double cream
salt and freshly ground black pepper
freshly grated nutmeg
1 egg yolk
15 g (½ oz) watercress, roughly
    chopped
4 mint leaves, roughly chopped
15 g (½ oz) Gruyère cheese, grated

To Garnish:
1 small tomato, skinned, seeded and
    diced
10 ml (2 tsp) chopped parsley

1 Steam the potatoes in their skins for 20 minutes, then place in cold water to cool for 5 minutes. Dry, peel, cut into 1 cm (½ inch) dice, and put to one side.

2 Use 5 g (¼ oz) of the butter to grease two 7 cm (2¾ inch) diameter metal ring moulds (see below). Melt 15 g (½ oz) of the butter in a pan, add the leek and onion and cook gently for 2 minutes.

3 Add the cream, bring to a rapid boil and boil for a few seconds. Remove from the heat and season with salt, pepper and nutmeg to taste.

4 Add the diced potato, egg yolk, watercress and mint. Mix together gently to avoid breaking up the potato dice.

5 Butter a large piece of foil with the remaining butter. (It must be large enough to wrap both rings.) Place the rings on the foil and two-thirds fill with the potato mixture. Top with the grated Gruyère.

6 Wrap the foil carefully around the rings to enclose, then steam for 15 minutes. Switch off the heat and allow the gâteaux to rest and settle for 5 minutes. Unmould onto warmed serving plates and garnish with tomato and parsley.

COOK'S TIP

If you don't have proper ring moulds, you could use small 300 g (10 oz) kidney bean tins with both ends removed. This is the ideal size.

WARM MUSHROOM AND BACON SALAD

15 ml (1 tbsp) olive oil
50 g (2 oz) smoked bacon, derinded and diced
1 garlic clove, crushed
25 g (1 oz) wild mushrooms, sliced
1 slice bread, cut into small cubes
50 g (2 oz) mixed salad leaves (frisée, lamb's lettuce, oakleaf lettuce etc)
2 small tomatoes, skinned, seeded and cut into julienne strips
25 g (1 oz) Bramley apple, peeled, cored and grated

Dressing:
15 g (½ oz) chopped onion
6 black peppercorns
25 ml (1 fl oz) each of tarragon and blackcurrant vinegars (home-made if possible, see below)
pinch of rosemary leaves
15 ml (1 tbsp) lime juice
25 ml (1 fl oz) crème de cassis
125 g (4 oz) unsalted butter
1 egg yolk
15 ml (1 tbsp) blackcurrant yogurt

1 Heat the oil in a frying pan and gently fry the bacon and garlic until the bacon is nearly crisp. Add the sliced mushrooms and bread cubes, and continue frying until the croûtons are brown and crisp. Drain on kitchen paper, and keep warm.

2 Mix the salad leaves with the tomato strips and grated apple, and leave to one side (only while you prepare the dressing, otherwise the apple will discolour).

3 For the dressing, put the onion, peppercorns, vinegars, rosemary, lime juice and cassis into a pan and reduce until only about 30 ml (2 tbsp) liquid remains in the pan; strain.

4 Melt the butter and carefully pour into a jug, leaving behind the white sediment – to yield clarified butter.

5 Put the egg yolk and strained vinegar reduction into a blender or food processor, and turn on to a slow speed. Add the butter slowly and when most of it is in, increase the speed to blend. Strain the sauce into a dish. Mix the yogurt in gently.

6 Toss the dressing with the leaves, and add the warm bacon mixture. Toss lightly and serve.

FLAVOURED VINEGARS

Flavoured vinegars may be difficult to buy, but they are very easy to make at home. Use a good wine vinegar as a base: mix 150 ml (¼ pint) white wine and 600 ml (1 pint) vinegar, and then add any fruits or herbs you desire. If using fruit, strain after 2 weeks and use; if using herbs, they can remain in the vinegar almost indefinitely. Do allow a minimum of 2 weeks, though, for the flavours to blend.

BREAD AND BUTTER PUDDING

25 g (1 oz) sultanas
90 ml (3 fl oz) Cointreau
50 g (2 oz) unsalted butter
1 Bramley apple, peeled, cored and
   chopped
50 g (2 oz) caster sugar
1 slice fresh root ginger
pinch of ground cinnamon
6 slices wholemeal brioche
3 egg yolks
90 ml (3 fl oz) double cream
¼ Cox's Pippin apple, peeled cored
   and sliced
finely grated rind of ½ lemon
25 g (1 oz) light brown sugar

Caramel Sauce:
20 ml (4 tsp) evaporated milk
20 ml (4 tsp) condensed milk
20 ml (4 tsp) vanilla sugar
2 ml (1 tsp) unsalted butter
10 ml (2 tsp) golden syrup
25 ml (1 fl oz) double cream

Ginger Anglaise:
2 egg yolks
10 ml (2 tsp) vanilla sugar
150 ml (¼ pint) milk

To Serve:
10 ml (2 tsp) clotted cream
seasonal fruit (apple and satsumas, or
   raspberries, blackberries, blueberries,
   passion fruit etc)
mint leaves

1 Put the sultanas and 50 ml (2 fl oz) of the Cointreau in a small bowl and leave to soak for at least 3 hours, or preferably overnight (or place in a steamer for 15 minutes).

2 Melt 15 g (½ oz) of the butter in a pan, and add the apple, 15 ml (1 tbsp) of the sugar, the ginger, cinnamon and 15 ml (1 tbsp) water. Cook gently until the apple is tender, then cool. Press through a sieve, discarding the ginger.

3 Butter 2 ramekins or similar-sized dishes. Sprinkle with a little of the remaining sugar to coat.

4 Cut the brioche slices to the shape of the dishes you are using, then place on a plate, and sprinkle with the rest of the Cointreau. Spread the remaining butter on the brioche slices.

5 Mix the egg yolks and cream together. Dip a slice of the buttered brioche into this and place in the bottom of one of the dishes. Place 5 ml (1 tsp) of the sultanas and 10 ml (2 tsp) sieved cooked apple on top. Place another dipped piece of brioche on top and press down lightly. Top with sultanas and apple, and finish with the third dipped slice of brioche. Do the same for the second dish.

6 Arrange the slices of Cox's Pippin in a fan shape on top of each dish. Mix half the lemon rind with the remaining caster sugar and half with the brown sugar. Sprinkle the apple with the lemon caster sugar, then the lemon brown sugar.

7 Stand the dishes in a bain-marie, or roasting tin containing enough hot water to come halfway up the sides of the dishes, and cook in the preheated oven at 170°C (340°F) mark 3-4 for 30 minutes.

8 For the caramel sauce, put all the ingredients into a small pan, and bring to the boil. Reduce the heat a little and cook, stirring often, until the sauce is golden brown. Remove from the heat and keep warm.

9 For the ginger anglaise, mix the egg yolks with the vanilla sugar in a bowl. Warm the milk in a heavy-based pan and, when nearly boiling, remove from the heat and pour on to the yolk mixture. Return to the clean pan and cook gently, stirring continuously, until the sauce is thick enough to coat the back of a spoon. Do not allow the sauce to boil.

10 Unmould the bread and butter puddings and place in the centre of each serving plate. Pour the warm caramel sauce to one side, the ginger Anglaise to the other. Put a spoonful of clotted cream on top of the pudding. Decorate with seasonal fruit and mint leaves. Serve at once.

Contestants
Katy Savage • Rebecca Beal • Katherine Smith

Panel of Judges
Nick Nairn • Anneka Rice • Loyd Grossman

Katherine Smith's Menu

MAIN COURSE
Chicken Breasts stuffed with Red Peppers
Catalonian Peppers
Pan-fried Potatoes with Fennel

DESSERT
Crema Catalan Ice Cream
"The flavour is just fantastic!" **Loyd**

Katherine Smith from York is 14 years old. Her parents own a sweet shop in the town centre and Katherine enjoys working there on Saturdays. She is an enthusiastic photographer and is currently taking part in a photographic course at York College. Katherine is also an expert on self-defence, holding a yellow belt in the martial art of Aikido.

CHICKEN BREASTS STUFFED WITH RED PEPPERS

2 medium chicken breasts, skinned and
  boned
75 ml (5 tbsp) plain flour
1 egg, beaten
120 ml (8 tbsp) ground almonds
15 ml (1 tbsp) roasted, blanched
  almonds, chopped
butter or oil, for shallow-frying

Red Pepper Stuffing:
1 large red pepper
1 onion
1 garlic clove
30 ml (2 tbsp) demerara sugar
15 ml (1 tbsp) red wine vinegar
7.5 ml (½ tbsp) olive oil
15 ml (1 tbsp) pine nuts

1 Make the red pepper stuffing well in advance as it has a better taste and texture when it has been refrigerated for several hours. Roughly chop the vegetables and then put everything, except the pine nuts, into a small saucepan over a low heat. Cook very gently for about 1½ hours until it has become a glossy, rich mixture. Allow to cool before adding the pine nuts. Chill until needed.

2 Carefully cut a large slit in the side of each chicken breast and fill with as much of the stuffing as possible. Secure the opening with cocktail sticks, then roll the chicken breasts in the flour. Next dip in the egg and finally coat the chicken breasts in the ground and chopped roasted almonds.

3 Heat the butter or oil in a large non-stick frying pan until it is gently bubbling, then carefully place each chicken piece in the pan. Fry over a medium heat for about 10 minutes, then turn over and fry the other side for 10 minutes. Both pieces should finish up a lovely golden-brown colour. Drain well on kitchen paper.

4 Serve immediately, with the Catalonian Peppers and Pan-fried Potatoes.

CATALONIAN PEPPERS

1 large red pepper
1 large yellow pepper
2 medium tomatoes, skinned
1 garlic clove, finely chopped
2 small anchovy fillets, finely chopped
40 ml (8 tsp) olive oil
salt and freshly ground black pepper

Baby Vegetable Filling:
5 baby carrots
5 baby sweetcorn
10 mangetouts
50 g (2 oz) butter
15 ml (1 tbsp) clear honey

1 Cut both peppers vertically in half and remove all seeds; leave the stalks on. Place the pepper halves on a greased baking sheet, skin-side down.

2 Cut the skinned tomatoes into quarters and place three or four pieces in each yellow pepper half, depending on how many can fit. Sprinkle the chopped garlic on top of the tomatoes, then the chopped anchovy.

3 Spoon over the olive oil, 10 ml (2 tsp) for each pepper half, then season the red pepper halves. Add a little pepper to the yellow pepper halves, but no salt (due to the anchovies).

4 Bake the peppers in a preheated oven at 200°C (400°F) mark 6 for 1 hour.

5 About 5 minutes before the peppers are ready, carefully chop up the baby vegetables. Heat the butter in a small frying pan until sizzling. Add the baby vegetables and stir-fry over a medium heat for 2-3 minutes until just beginning to brown, then add the honey. Continue to stir-fry until the honey has melted, then remove from the heat.

6 Delicately fill the red pepper halves with the baby vegetables. Pour the honey and butter juices over the top. Serve immediately, one half of each colour pepper for each person.

Salmon and Plaice Twists with a Smoked Salmon and Coriander Sauce
CLARE ENGEL'S MAIN COURSE (Regional Heat)

Bread and Butter Pudding with a Caramel Sauce and Ginger Anglaise
REBECCA BEAL'S DESSERT (Regional Heat)

PAN-FRIED POTATOES WITH FENNEL

450 g (1 lb) new potatoes
45 ml (3 tbsp) vegetable oil
5 ml (1 tsp) fennel seeds
salt

1 Scrub and rinse the potatoes and pat dry. If they are large, cut them into large dice, but leave the skins on.

2 Heat the oil in a large wok to a very high temperature, then add the potatoes. Give them a stir to coat with the oil, then sprinkle on the fennel seeds and some salt.

3 Cook the potatoes, stirring frequently, for 20-30 minutes until they are really well done, crisp round the edges and golden brown in the middle. Drain on kitchen paper and serve immediately.

CREMA CATALAN ICE CREAM

2 egg yolks
50 g (2 oz) caster sugar
150 ml (¼ pint) milk
150 ml (¼ pint) double cream, whipped
5 ml (1 tsp) vanilla essence
5 ml (1 tsp) freshly grated nutmeg
60 ml (4 tbsp) demerara sugar

1 Whisk the egg yolks and sugar together in a bowl. Meanwhile heat the milk in a heavy-based pan over a low heat. When the milk reaches boiling point, pour it onto the whisked yolk mixture, whisking constantly. Return to the saucepan and cook over a low heat, stirring constantly, until the custard is thicken enough to coat the back of the spoon. Remove from the heat and allow to cool.

2 When the custard is cold, fold in the whipped cream, vanilla essence and nutmeg. Pour the mixture into an ice-cream maker and churn until almost frozen. Alternatively, freeze the mixture in a shallow freezerproof container, whisking periodically during freezing to break down the ice crystals.

3 Divide the mixture between 2 ramekins or crema catalan dishes, smooth the surface and place in the freezer to firm up.

4 When the ice cream has frozen solid, preheat the grill to high. Sprinkle 30 ml (2 tbsp) demerara sugar over each ice cream and quickly put under the heat to caramelise.

5 If the ice cream melts under the grill, return to the freezer for a while. Otherwise serve immediately.

Contestants
Graham Booth • Lauren Addison • David Watkinson

Panel of Judges
David Wilson • Dani Behr • Loyd Grossman

WINNER

Graham Booth's Menu

MAIN COURSE
Duck Breast stuffed with Prunes and Apple served with
a Sherry and Redcurrant Sauce
"Absolutely delicious duck" **Dani Behr**
Pan-fried Garlic Potatoes
Timbales of Spinach and Carrot

DESSERT
Pears on a Biscuit Base with a Lemon and Butterscotch Sauce
"The sauce and biscuit work well together" **David Wilson**

Eleven year old Graham Booth comes from Woodbridge in Suffolk. Graham's mother is a music teacher, and he seems to have inherited her talents. Having mastered the violin and trombone, Graham is now tackling the bassoon. He is also an extremely keen cricketer and is now training with the Suffolk County under-12 squad. Graham enjoys drama as well and recently played the Artful Dodger in his school's production of the Dickens classic, *Oliver Twist*.

DUCK BREASTS STUFFED WITH PRUNES AND APPLE, SERVED WITH A SHERRY AND REDCURRANT SAUCE

2 boneless duck breasts, each about 225 g (8 oz)
1 cooking apple
100 g (3½ oz) stoned prunes (ready-soaked)
salt and freshly ground black pepper
125 ml (4 fl oz) medium sherry
30 ml (2 tbsp) redcurrant jelly

To Garnish:
watercress or parsley sprigs

1 Wash the duck breasts and pat dry with kitchen paper. Make a slit in each breast with a sharp knife.

2 Peel, core and finely chop the apple. Chop the prunes and mix with the apple. Stuff each duck breast with this mixture. Season the skins with plenty of salt and pepper.

3 Put the duck breasts on a rack over a baking tin and bake in a preheated oven at 220°C (425°F) mark 7 for 50 minutes - 1 hour. When ready, transfer the duck breasts to a plate and keep warm.

4 Skim off the fat from the juices in the baking tin, and add the sherry and redcurrant jelly. Simmer on top of the cooker, stirring until smooth and slightly reduced.

5 Spoon some of the sauce over the duck breasts and serve the remainder separately in a sauceboat. Garnish with watercress or parsley and serve with the vegetable accompaniments.

ROASTING DUCK BREASTS

To encourage the duck to release fat during roasting, score the skin with a sharp knife before cooking. Roasting the duck breasts on a wire rack enables the fat to drip into the pan below and helps the skin to crisp up.

PAN-FRIED GARLIC POTATOES

6-10 small new potatoes
salt and freshly ground black pepper
30 ml (2 tbsp) oil
7.5 ml (½ tbsp) butter
1 garlic clove, crushed

1 Boil the potatoes in their skins in lightly salted water for about 10-15 minutes until just tender. Drain and set aside.

2 Heat the oil and butter in a frying pan until bubbling, add the garlic and stir. Add the potatoes and stir over heat for 1-2 minutes. Drain, season to taste, and serve.

TIMBALES OF SPINACH AND CARROT

125 g (4 oz) spinach, trimmed and
  chopped
125 g (4 oz) carrots, grated
15 g (½ oz) butter, melted
2 pinches of freshly grated nutmeg
salt and freshly ground black pepper

1 Steam the spinach and grated carrot over a pan of boiling water for 2 minutes. Drain thoroughly and press firmly between two plates to remove excess liquid.

2 Mix the vegetables with the melted butter, nutmeg and seasoning to taste. Grease 2 timbale moulds and fill with the spinach and carrot mixture.

3 Place on a baking sheet in a preheated oven at 220°C (425°F) mark 7 for 5 minutes. Unmould and serve immediately.

PEARS ON A BISCUIT BASE WITH A LEMON AND BUTTERSCOTCH SAUCE

1 pear, red skinned if possible
juice of 1 lemon
25 g (1 oz) brown sugar
25 g (1 oz) fromage frais

Base:
100 g (3½ oz) plain chocolate
   digestive biscuits
50 g (2 oz) butter

Sauce:
250 ml (8 fl oz) sugar
60 ml (4 tbsp) water
juice of 2 lemons
50 g (2 oz) salted butter
125 ml (4 fl oz) double cream

To Decorate:
lemon or orange leaves

1 First make the sauce. Melt the sugar in a heavy-based saucepan over a low heat. Increase the heat to medium and cook until the sugar caramelises. Carefully add the water, lemon juice, butter and cream, standing well back as the mixture will splutter. Stir until smooth, then set aside.

2 For the base, crush the biscuits in a blender or food processor. Melt the butter in a saucepan over a gentle heat and stir in the biscuit crumbs. Press evenly into 2 pear-shaped cutters and place on a greased tray or non-stick base from a cake tin. Chill.

3 Poach the pear in enough water to cover, with the lemon juice and brown sugar added, for 10 minutes or until tender. Set aside to cool.

4 To assemble, halve the pear and scoop out the centre with a melon baller. Fill the cavities with the fromage frais. Slide the chilled biscuit bases on to plates and place the pears on top, cavities down.

5 Pour the lemon and butterscotch sauce around the pears, and decorate the plate with lemon or orange leaves.

REGIONAL HEATS
The East

Contestants
Graham Booth • Lauren Addison • David Watkinson

Panel of Judges
David Wilson • Dani Behr • Loyd Grossman

Lauren Addison's Menu

MAIN COURSE
Seafood Paella
Leaf Salad tossed in Olive Oil Dressing

DESSERT
Compote of Cinnamon-scented Autumn and Winter Fruits
Spiced Orange Shortbread Biscuits
"Sharp and spicy" **Loyd**

One of the youngest competitors, 10 year old Lauren
Addison lives in Norwich where her family run a
restaurant, in the city centre – named Loyd's. Lauren is
currently learning to play the clarinet. She is also keen on
sports and has already won an ASA gold medal for her
javelin throwing. Lauren is also a football fanatic –
supporting Manchester United, and playing for a team
known as The Red Roses.

SEAFOOD PAELLA

30 ml (2 tbsp) extra-virgin olive oil
½ large Spanish onion, chopped
2 large garlic cloves, chopped
175 g (6 oz) arborio rice
1.2 litres (2 pints) fish stock
1 sachet saffron threads
pinch of paprika
salt and freshly ground black pepper
4 cooked Dublin Bay prawns in shell
  (optional)
4 cooked large prawns in shell
4 small squid
600 ml (1 pint) mussels in shell
50 g (2 oz) green beans, trimmed

1 Heat half the olive oil in a paella pan or heavy-based pan, add the onion and garlic and fry gently until soft but not brown.

2 Add the rice and fry, stirring, for 1-2 minutes. Add three quarters of the stock, the saffron, paprika, salt and pepper. Simmer gently for about 45 minutes; stir occasionally, adding more stock if necessary.

3 Meanwhile, prepare the shellfish. Shell the Dublin Bay prawns and large prawns, and remove the dark intestinal vein that runs along the back. Clean the squid, discarding the skin and slice into rings. Rinse the mussels thoroughly, removing their beards, and discard any with open or damaged shells.

4 Blanch the green beans in boiling salted water for a minute or so, and stir into the rice.

5 Steam the mussels in a little of the remaining seasoned stock in a tightly covered pan, shaking the pan occasionally, for 3-5 minutes until the shells have opened. Discard any mussels which have not opened. Remove and discard the empty top shells. Heat the remaining olive oil in a pan, add all the prawns and squid and sauté for a few minutes to heat through.

6 Arrange the prawns and squid on top of the rice and the mussels in a circle around them. Cover with a lid or foil and leave on a low heat or in a low oven until ready to serve.

LEAF SALAD TOSSED IN OLIVE OIL DRESSING

*a handful of mixed green and red
    salad leaves*

Dressing:
*1 garlic clove, crushed
salt and freshly ground black pepper
pinch of sugar
pinch of dry mustard
60 ml (4 tbsp) olive oil
15 ml (1 tbsp) sherry vinegar
    (approximately)*

1 Wash the salad leaves and drain. Put into a plastic bag in the refrigerator to crisp up.

2 For the dressing, put the garlic, salt, pepper, sugar, mustard, olive oil, and sherry vinegar to taste in a screw-topped jar. Shake vigorously to combine.

3 Just before serving, put the salad leaves in a salad bowl, pour on the dressing and toss gently.

SALAD LEAVES

Use any combination of crisp colourful leaves, such as frisée, lamb's lettuce, oakleaf lettuce and radicchio. Bags of mixed ready-prepared salad leaves – available from supermarkets – are a convenient way of buying salad leaves if you only need a small quantity.

COMPOTE OF CINNAMON-SCENTED AUTUMN AND WINTER FRUITS

1 small pear
1 small Cox's apple
2-3 red plums
50 g (2 oz) elderberries
50 g (2 oz) blackberries
50 g (2 oz) cranberries
50 g (2 oz) sugar (or to taste)
15-30 ml (1-2 tbsp) water
1 cinnamon stick

To Serve:
30-60 ml (2-4 tbsp) sweetened fromage
 frais (optional)
Spiced Orange Shortbread Biscuits

1 Peel and chop the pear and apple. Stone the plums.

2 Place all the fruit, the sugar, water and cinnamon stick in a heavy-based saucepan. Cover with the lid and stew gently until the fruit is tender, about 10 minutes. Leave to cool.

3 Serve the compote in a glass dish accompanied by sweetened fromage frais if using, and the shortbread biscuits.

SWEETENED FROMAGE FRAIS
Sweeten the fromage frais with a little sugar or honey. If you have some mild scented honey, use this – to impart a delicate flavour.

SPICED ORANGE SHORTBREAD BISCUITS

75 g (3 oz) plain flour
large pinch of ground cinnamon
40 g (1½ oz) caster sugar
25 g (1 oz) ground rice
finely grated rind of 1 orange
75 g (3 oz) butter, diced

1 Sift the flour and cinnamon together into a bowl. Stir in the sugar, ground rice and orange rind. Rub in the butter until the mixture resembles fine breadcrumbs. Knead until the dough forms a smooth ball. (Alternatively, mix together in a food processor.)

2 Roll out the dough to a 3 mm (⅛ inch) thickness and cut into shapes, using a suitable biscuit cutter. Place on a lightly greased baking sheet.

3 Bake in a preheated oven at 160°C (325°F) mark 3 for 10 minutes or until golden. Leave to cool, then transfer to a serving plate.

Contestants

Graham Booth • Lauren Addison • David Watkinson

Panel of Judges

David Wilson • Dani Behr • Loyd Grossman

David Watkinson's Menu

MAIN COURSE

Greek-style Pork with Fresh Herb Fettucine and
Sweet Pepper Sauce

DESSERT

Mango and Kumquat Refresher

"Very refreshing and gave a nice aftertaste" **Dani Behr**

David Watkinson comes from Great Barton in Suffolk and is 13 years old. David has recently taken up rifle shooting, and has joined a club in Bury St Edmunds. He is also an enthusiastic table tennis player. Both David and his mother are keen on mushroom collecting and take every opportunity to gather wild mushrooms from the woods near their home.

GREEK-STYLE PORK WITH FRESH HERB FETTUCINE AND SWEET PEPPER SAUCE

1 pork fillet, about 350 g (12 oz)
15 ml (1 tbsp) seasoned plain flour
6-8 green or black olives, pitted
about 50 g (2 oz) Feta cheese
30 ml (2 tbsp) olive oil

Marinade:
60 ml (4 tbsp) olive oil
15 ml (1 tbsp) wine vinegar or lemon juice
bouquet garni (parsley, oregano, basil etc)
few black peppercorns

Herb Fettucine:
large handful of fresh herbs (parsley, chives, basil etc)
125 g (4 oz) strong plain flour (or 75 g (3 oz) plain flour plus 25 g (1 oz) Durum wheat semolina flour)
1 egg (size 3)
15 ml (1 tbsp) water
15 ml (1 tbsp) olive oil

Sweet Pepper Sauce:
1½-2 red peppers
3 very ripe tomatoes (or 2 tinned plum tomatoes)
45 ml (3 tbsp) white wine (approximately)
5 ml (1 tsp) brown sugar
1.25 ml (¼ tsp) paprika

1 Make a lengthwise slit along the pork fillet, without cutting right through, then place in a shallow dish. Mix together the marinade ingredients, pour over the meat and turn to coat on all sides. Leave to marinate in a cool place for 24 hours.

2 To make the fettucine, put the herbs into a food processor and process until finely chopped. Remove half the herbs and set aside. Add the flour, egg, water and oil to the machine and blend for 3 minutes. Remove the dough from the machine and knead on a lightly floured surface for 1 minute. Wrap in cling film and leave to rest for at least 30 minutes.

3 Roll out the pasta to a very thin large sheet. Roll up loosely and cut into long ribbon strips. Carefully unravel the strips and leave the fettucine to dry a little, on a clean floured tea-towel.

4 Remove the pork from the marinade, strain the marinade and reserve. Cut the Feta cheese into tiny chunks and use to stuff the olives. Push the stuffed olives one by one into the slit in the pork. Secure with cocktail sticks or tie the stuffed pork fillet at intervals with cotton string. Dust the pork all over with the seasoned flour.

5 Heat the olive oil in a frying pan, add the pork and fry quickly over a high heat for 30 seconds, turning to seal on all sides. Transfer to an oven-proof dish and spoon over the oil and reserved marinade. Cook in a preheated oven at 220°C (425°F) mark 7 for 20 minutes, basting once. (Stand a dish of water in the bottom of the oven for moisture.)

6 Meanwhile, make the sauce. Halve and deseed the peppers and tomatoes; roughly chop the flesh. Place in a saucepan together with all the remaining sauce ingredients. Bring to a simmer and cook gently for 20 minutes. Transfer to a food processor or blender and work to a purée, then pass through a sieve. Add a little more wine if the sauce is too thick.

7 When the pork is ready, leave to rest in a warm place for 5 minutes, then carve into slices. Meanwhile, cook the fettucine in a large pan of boiling salted water for a few minutes until *al dente* (tender but firm to the bite); drain well. Reheat the sweet pepper sauce.

8 To serve, pool the sauce on warmed serving plates, and fan the pork slices on top to display the stuffing. Place a pile of fettucine at one side and sprinkle with the remaining chopped herbs.

MANGO AND KUMQUAT REFRESHER

1 large mango
6-8 kumquats
15 ml (1 tbsp) caster sugar
10 ml (2 tsp) powdered gelatine
45 ml (3 tbsp) lemon juice

Ginger Cream:
150 ml (¼ pint) double cream
5 ml (1 tsp) caster sugar
15 ml (1 tbsp) Grand Marnier or Cointreau
2 pieces preserved stem ginger in syrup, drained and finely chopped

To Decorate:
15 ml (1 tbsp) chopped pistachio nuts
2 kumquats, sliced
2 mint leaves

1 Peel and stone the mango; roughly chop the flesh. Cut the kumquats in half and remove the seeds. Put the fruit (kumquat skins as well) and sugar in a food processor or blender and process until smooth.

2 Soak the gelatine in the lemon juice in a small heatproof bowl, then place over a pan of hot water until dissolved.

3 Add the dissolved gelatine to the fruit purée and mix well. Spoon into 2 dampened 10 cm (4 inch) individual ring moulds and refrigerate until set.

4 Meanwhile prepare the ginger cream. Whip the cream with the sugar until thick, then add the liqueur. Fold in the chopped ginger.

5 Briefly dip the moulds in hot water and unmould the desserts on to plates. Fill the centres with the flavoured cream. Sprinkle with the chopped pistachios and decorate each plate with kumquat slices and mint leaves.

The Home Counties

Contestants
Nicola Trundle • Helen Deacon • Kirsty Kempster

Panel of Judges
Ainsley Harriott • Duncan Goodhew • Loyd Grossman

WINNER

Nicola Trundle's Menu

MAIN COURSE
Bream in Red Wine Sauce with Porcini, Leeks and Beef Marrow
"I was very impressed with the bream" **Ainsley Harriott**
"Absolutely spectacular" **Loyd**

DESSERT
Chestnut and Chocolate Mousse
"Light, nice, very pleasant on the tongue" **Ainsley Harriott**

Thirteen year old Nicola Trundle comes from Maidenhead in Berkshire and is a boarder at Pipers Corner School in High Wycombe. Her varied interests include playing the flute, shooting and drama. She recently performed in the school's production of *Daisy Pulls it Off*.

BREAM IN RED WINE SAUCE WITH PORCINI, LEEKS AND BEEF MARROW

2 sea bream steaks, each about 225 g (8 oz), trimmed
50 g (2 oz) porcini (dried mushrooms)
2 slices beef marrow
3 leeks, trimmed and thickly sliced
50 g (2 oz) butter

Sauce:
300 ml (½ pint) red wine
fish trimmings (head, bones etc)
2 shallots, finely chopped
50 g (2 oz) butter
20 ml (1½ tbsp) tomato purée
pinch of sugar
juice of ¼ lemon

1 Soak the porcini in sufficient cold water to cover for 3 hours before starting.

2 For the sauce, put the wine and fish trimmings into a pan. Bring to the boil and simmer, uncovered, for 20 minutes.

3 Fry the shallots in 15 g (½ oz) of the butter until soft and golden, then strain the reduced wine into the pan. Add the tomato purée and simmer to reduce by two thirds.

4 Strain the sauce to remove the shallots, then poach the beef marrow in the liquid for 8 minutes. Remove the beef marrow slices and keep warm.

5 Cook the leeks and porcini, each with a knob of butter, and separately, for 5 minutes. Drain the leeks. Add 45-60 ml (3-4 tbsp) of the porcini juice to the sauce, then drain the porcini. Keep the leeks and porcini warm.

6 Season the sauce with salt, pepper, a little sugar and the lemon juice. Beat in the remaining butter, a piece at a time.

7 To cook the fish steaks, heat the remaining butter in a frying pan, add the fish and cook for 3-5 minutes only on each side until golden and just cooked. Pour the sauce over half of each warmed serving plate and place the fish on top. Arrange the leek pieces around the fish and put the porcini to one side, with the marrow slice on top. Serve at once.

CHESTNUT AND CHOCOLATE MOUSSE

225 g (8 oz) can unsweetened chestnut
  purée
15 g (½ oz) butter
15 ml (1 tbsp) golden syrup
2 small trifle sponges
15 ml (1 tbsp) brandy
60 g (2½ oz) plain chocolate, broken
  into pieces
150 ml (¼ pint) double cream

1 Put the chestnut purée in a bowl and mash until smooth.

2 Melt the butter and syrup together in a small pan over a low heat, then add to the chestnut purée. Mix well.

3 Crumble the trifle sponges into a small dish, sprinkle with the brandy and leave to soak.

4 Melt 50 g (2 oz) of the chocolate in a bowl over a pan of hot water. In another bowl, whip half the cream until soft peaks form.

5 Add the chestnut purée to the trifle sponges and mix until smooth. Fold in the chocolate and whipped cream until evenly incorporated.

6 Divide the mixture between ramekins. Whip the remaining cream and use to cover the mousses. Grate the remaining chocolate over the mousses to decorate. Chill in the refrigerator for 1 hour before serving.

Contestants
Nicola Trundle • Helen Deacon • Kirsty Kempster

Panel of Judges
Ainsley Harriott • Duncan Goodhew • Loyd Grossman

Helen Deacon's Menu

MAIN COURSE
Chicken Roulé with a Sun-dried Tomato and Mushroom Stuffing
Carrot and Orange Timbales
Tarragon Stoved Potatoes
Sugar Snap Peas
"Very inventive" **Ainsley Harriott**

DESSERT
Chocolate Marquise with a Crème de Menthe Sauce
"I loved the rich bitter chocolate taste" **Ainsley Harriott**

From Woking in Surrey, Helen Deacon is 15 years old. Helen attends Tormead School, where she is a keen member of the Young Engineers Club. She's also an enthusiastic skier. As part of the community service for her Duke of Edinburgh Silver Award, Helen helps look after the animals at the Burpham Rare Breeds Farm.

CHICKEN ROULÉ WITH A SUN-DRIED TOMATO AND MUSHROOM STUFFING, SERVED WITH A LEMON SAUCE

2 boneless chicken breasts, skinned
75 g (3 oz) shiitake mushrooms, finely chopped
2 shallots, finely chopped
6 sun-dried tomato pieces in oil, drained and finely chopped
90 ml (6 tbsp) white wine
4 rashers lightly smoked streaky bacon
salt and freshly ground black pepper
a little butter
30 ml (2 tbsp) chicken stock

Lemon Sauce:
30 g (1¼ oz) butter
7.5 ml (½ tbsp) plain flour
60 ml (2 fl oz) chicken stock
30 ml (2 tbsp) lemon juice
60 ml (2 fl oz) double cream

1 For the stuffing, put the mushrooms, shallots and sun-dried tomatoes in a small pan with 60 ml (4 tbsp) of the wine and cook for about 5 minutes until the shallots are softened.

2 Place the chicken breasts between layers of cling film and beat with a mallet until flattened to about a 1 cm (½ inch) thickness.

3 Divide the mushroom mixture between the chicken breasts, spreading it to 2 cm (¾ inch) from the edge. Roll each breast up fairly tightly, like a Swiss roll. Wrap each in 2 rashers of streaky bacon to hold them together.

4 Place each roll on a piece of foil, season and add a knob of butter. Add 15 ml (1 tbsp) wine and 15 ml (1 tbsp) stock to each parcel and wrap the foil around the chicken to enclose.

5 Place on a baking sheet and cook in a preheated oven at 200°C (400°F) mark 6 for 45 minutes until tender. Turn off the oven and leave to rest inside the oven for 10 minutes.

6 Meanwhile, make the sauce. Melt the butter in a pan and add the flour; stir well to a smooth paste and cook for 30 seconds. Gradually add the chicken stock and lemon juice, stirring continuously. Bring to the boil, and simmer for 3 minutes. Reduce the heat and stir in the cream. Heat gently; do not boil.

7 Slice the chicken rolls and arrange on warmed serving plates to reveal the swirls of stuffing. Serve with the sauce and accompaniments.

CARROT AND ORANGE TIMBALES

2-3 medium carrots
5 ml (1 tsp) finely grated orange rind
pinch of freshly grated nutmeg
salt and freshly ground black pepper
2 knobs of butter

1 Coarsely grate the carrots using a food processor if possible, then mix together with the orange rind, nutmeg and seasoning.

2 Spoon into 2 non-metallic ramekin dishes and press well down. Add a knob of butter to each. Microwave on high for 2 minutes. (Alternatively put them in the turned-off oven with the chicken for 10 minutes to heat through.)

TARRAGON STOVED POTATOES

14 baby new potatoes, washed
few tarragon sprigs, roughly chopped
120 ml (4 fl oz) chicken stock

1 Put the potatoes in a non-stick saucepan, and add the tarragon and chicken stock. Put the lid on, bring to the boil, then turn the heat right down to its lowest setting.

2 Cook gently, shaking the covered pan every few minutes to prevent sticking, for 25 minutes. Drain and serve.

CHOCOLATE MARQUISE WITH A CREME DE MENTHE SAUCE

20 g (¾ oz) plain chocolate, broken
  into pieces
1 egg yolk
35 g (1¼ oz) caster sugar
25 g (1 oz) cocoa powder, sifted
45 g (1¾ oz) butter, softened
75 ml (2½ fl oz) whipping cream
10 g (a good ¼ oz) icing sugar

Sauce:
60 ml (2 fl oz) double cream
60 ml (2 fl oz) milk
1 egg yolk
15 g (½ oz) caster sugar
40 ml (2½ tbsp) green crème de menthe

1 Melt the chocolate in a heatproof bowl over a pan of hot water. Allow to cool slightly.

2 Whisk the egg yolk with the sugar until thick, pale and creamy. Fold the melted chocolate into the whisked yolk and sugar mixture.

3 In a separate bowl, mix the cocoa powder with the soft butter to a smooth cream. Add this to the chocolate mixture.

4 Whisk the whipping cream with the icing sugar until it just holds its shape. Add to the chocolate mixture and whisk briskly until evenly blended.

5 Line a small loaf tin (or any appropriate mould) with cling film and spoon in the mousse mixture. Put into the freezer for 30 minutes to chill (no longer, or it will freeze).

6 Meanwhile, make the sauce. Heat the cream and milk together in a saucepan until just boiling. Mix the egg yolk and sugar together in a bowl. Pour the milk and cream on to the egg yolk mixture, whisking constantly. Pour back into the pan and heat gently, stirring constantly, until the sauce is thick enough to coat the back of the spoon. Take off the heat, and add the crème de menthe. Cool.

7 To serve, turn the marquise out of the tin and cut into slices, about 2 cm (¾ inch) thick. Pour some green sauce onto each plate and place a slice of marquise on top.

REGIONAL HEATS
The Home Counties

Contestants
Nicola Trundle • Helen Deacon • Kirsty Kempster

Panel of Judges
Ainsley Harriott • Duncan Goodhew • Loyd Grossman

Kirsty Kempster's Menu

MAIN COURSE
Chicken enveloped in Smoked Bacon
Vegetable Parcels
New Potatoes
"Marvellous balance between the sweet and the bitter"
"The sauce was delicate and light" **Ainsley Harriott**

DESSERT
Raspberry and Redcurrant Hazelnut Meringues
"I loved those meringues" **Duncan Goodhew**

Fourteen-year-old Kirsty Kempster comes from Weybridge in Surrey. Kirsty attends Surbiton High School where chemistry is her favourite subject. Her extra-curricula activities include visiting housebound local pensioners, with her friends.

CHICKEN ENVELOPED IN SMOKED BACON

4 chicken thighs
15 g (½ oz) butter
½ onion, thinly sliced
4 smoked bacon rashers
salt and freshly ground black pepper
300 ml (½ pint) chicken stock (plus more if needed)
15-20 ml (1-1½ tbsp) chopped tarragon
30-45 ml (2-3 tbsp) crème fraîche

To Garnish:
tarragon leaves

1 Melt the butter in a lidded frying pan over a low heat, add the onion and cook gently until very soft.

2 Meanwhile, skin and bone the chicken thighs, then wrap a bacon rasher around each chicken thigh.

3 Season the onions with salt and pepper, and place the wrapped chicken thighs on top. Add the chicken stock and sprinkle the chicken with chopped tarragon. Cover the pan with the lid and simmer gently for 50 minutes, adding more stock if necessary.

4 Take the chicken pieces out of the pan, and keep them warm. Strain the remaining sauce into a saucepan and add the crème fraîche. Mix over a very low heat.

5 Serve the chicken with the sauce and a sprinkling of fresh tarragon.

VEGETABLE PARCELS

2 large Savoy cabbage leaves
8 fine green beans
½ carrot
¼ leek, white part only, cleaned
½ courgette

1 Blanch the cabbage leaves in boiling water for 30 seconds and use to line 2 ramekin dishes allowing the leaves to overhang the sides.

2 Top and tail the beans and cut them in half. Peel and slice the carrot into matchsticks, about the same size as the beans. Blanch the carrot and beans in boiling water for 3 minutes.

3 Cut the leek into matchsticks, the same length as the beans. Cut the courgette into matchsticks of the same length. Blanch the courgette and leek for 1 minute.

4 Place half the vegetables in one of the cabbage-lined ramekins, and fold the leaf over to enclose them. Cover the top with foil. Repeat with the other ramekin.

5 Stand the ramekins in a shallow pan containing enough boiling water to come halfway up the sides and steam for 30 minutes. Lift out the ramekins and turn the parcels out on to warmed serving plates.

RASPBERRY AND REDCURRANT HAZELNUT MERINGUES

1 egg white
50 g (2 oz) caster sugar
few drops of vanilla essence
1.25 ml (¼ tsp) white wine vinegar
25 g (1 oz) roasted chopped hazelnuts

Filling:
50 g (2 oz) raspberries
50 g (2 oz) redcurrants
75 ml (5 tbsp) double cream, whipped

To Decorate:
icing sugar, for dusting
2 redcurrant sprigs

1 Whisk the egg white until stiff, then add the caster sugar a spoonful at a time, beating constantly. Beat in the vanilla essence and vinegar, then fold in the hazelnuts.

2 On a baking sheet lined with non-stick baking parchment, draw four 7.5 cm (3 inch) circles. Divide the meringue mixture between the circles, smoothing it to the edges.

3 Cook in a preheated oven at 170°C (340°F) mark 3-4 for 15 minutes or until the meringue circles are golden. Take out of the oven and leave to cool.

4 Put the raspberries and 25 g (1 oz) of the redcurrants in a nylon sieve over a bowl and crush with the back of a wooden spoon. Leave the liquid purée to one side, and mix the crushed raspberry and redcurrants left in the sieve with the whipped cream.

5 Invert one meringue circle onto an individual serving plate. Cover with half of the cream and half of the remaining whole redcurrants. Sandwich together with another meringue round. Repeat with the other meringues, cream and redcurrants.

6 Sprinkle icing sugar over the meringues and decorate with sprigs of redcurrants. Serve the fruit purée as an accompanying sauce.

REGIONAL HEATS
The North West

Contestants
Shabab Hashmie • Danielle Crowley • Sam Goss

Panel of Judges
Antony Worrall-Thompson • Lee Chapman • Loyd Grossman

WINNER

Shabab Hashmie's Menu

MAIN COURSE
Chicken Tikka Masala

Pilau Rice

"Excellent" **Antony Worrall-Thompson**

DESSERT
Firnie (Asian Ground Rice Pudding)

"My favourite dessert" **Lee Chapman**

"A chic pudding" **Loyd**

Shabab Hashmie is 13 years of age and comes from Rochdale. Shabab is no stranger to television as she has appeared, together with her brother Shabaz, on a number of programmes playing Indian music. All the family are devout Muslims and spend time each day reading from the Koran. Shabab's newest enthusiasm is canoeing and she often ventures out on nearby Hollingworth Lake with her brother.

CHICKEN TIKKA MASALA

*2 chicken breast fillets, skinned and
diced*

Marinade:
*120-150 ml (8-10 tbsp) natural yogurt
45 ml (3 tbsp) vegetable oil
salt
5 ml (1 tsp) each of ground coriander
and chilli powder
2.5 ml (½ tsp) turmeric*

Sauce:
*2 large onions, quartered
400 ml (14 fl oz) water
100 ml (3½ fl oz) vegetable oil
1 green chilli, halved and seeded
1 green pepper, halved, cored and
seeded
1 cinnamon stick
2 cloves
1 black and 1 green cardamom
5 ml (1 tsp) each of chilli powder and
ground coriander
1.25 ml (¼ tsp) turmeric
a little red food colouring
30 ml (2 tbsp) desiccated coconut*

1 About 6 hours before you wish to cook, mix together the ingredients for the marinade in a bowl. Add the chicken and turn to coat thoroughly. Cover and leave to marinate in the refrigerator.

2 Remove the chicken from the marinade after its 6 hours, drain well and set aside. Pour the marinade into a saucepan and simmer gently for about 15-20 minutes.

3 For the sauce, put the onions, water and oil in a pan and cook gently for 15-20 minutes until the onions are tender. Pour into a blender or food processor, add the chilli and green pepper, and work to a purée. Pour back into the pan and add the whole spices, the ground spices and a little food colouring, plus 5 ml (1 tsp) salt. Cook gently for 10-11 minutes.

4 Place the reduced marinade in a large frying pan and add a few ladlefuls of the sauce, depending on how thin you want your sauce. Remove the whole spices. Add the chicken and cook over a gentle heat for at least 15-20 minutes.

5 Sprinkle with the desiccated coconut and cook for a further 2-3 minutes on a medium heat. Serve with Pilau Rice (see overleaf).

PILAU RICE

225 g (8 oz) basmati rice
red food colouring
15 ml (1 tbsp) clarified butter

1 Wash the rice well in a sieve under cold running water, then leave to soak in a bowl of cold water for 15-20 minutes. Drain well.

2 Place the drained rice in a pan and pour in enough boiling water to cover it by at least 1 cm (½ inch). Simmer over a medium heat until the rice has absorbed the water; it will be half cooked at this stage.

3 At one side of the rice, about 1-2 cm (½ -¾ inch) in from the side of the pan, put a blob of the red food colouring. Put a teatowel over the top of the pan, being careful not to let its ends trail on to the hot gas or electric rings, and cover tightly with the lid. Simmer on the very gentlest heat possible to allow the rice to steam and finish its cooking, about 15 minutes.

4 Add the clarified butter to the rice and fluff it up, so that the grains glisten and the food colouring is roughly distributed. Serve hot.

BASMATI RICE

Basmati rice is prized for its long, slender grains and fine flavour. Rinsing and soaking the rice before cooking is essential for optimum results.

FIRNIE (ASIAN GROUND RICE PUDDING)

600 ml (1 pint) milk
75 ml (5 tbsp) ground rice
45 ml (3 tbsp) caster sugar
edible silver leaf (vark), to decorate

1 Bring three quarters of the milk to the boil in a saucepan over a medium heat.

2 While the milk is coming to the boil, put the remaining cold milk in a mixing bowl with the ground rice and sugar. Mix well, then stir into the boiled milk.

3 Mix to prevent any lumps forming, and stir continuously over a gentle heat until the mixture has thickened. Pour into serving dishes and refrigerate to cool.

4 Serve cool, decorated with the silver leaf.

SILVER LEAF

This unusual ingredient is unique to Indian cooking. It is made by beating tiny pellets of silver into paper-thin sheets, and is used to garnish festive meat and rice dishes as well as desserts.

REGIONAL HEATS
The North West

Contestants
Shabab Hashmie • Danielle Crowley • Sam Goss

Panel of Judges
Antony Worrall-Thompson • Lee Chapman • Loyd Grossman

Danielle Crowley's Menu

MAIN COURSE
Medallions of Lamb in a Port Sauce
Fan-roasted Potatoes
Glazed Carrots
Tarragon Leeks
"Flavours work very well" **Lee Chapman**

DESSERT
Chocolate Mousse, served in Biscuit Cups
"Good flavour" **Antony Worrall-Thompson**

Danielle Crowley is ten years old and comes from Chaddesden in Derbyshire. Danielle attends Cherry Tree Junior School where she's an enthusiastic member of the chess club. Danielle also loves climbing, and regularly climbs with her friends around Black Rock which overlooks nearby Matlock. She also enjoys roller discos.

MEDALLIONS OF LAMB IN A PORT SAUCE

350 g (12 oz) lamb fillet
15 ml (1 tbsp) olive oil
15 ml (1 tbsp) redcurrant jelly
150 ml (¼ pint) ruby port
300 ml (½ pint) beef stock
150 ml (¼ pint) double cream
salt and freshly ground black pepper

1 Heat the olive oil in a heavy-based frying pan and, when hot, add the fillet of lamb in one piece. Cook over a high heat, turning to seal quickly all over.

2 When sealed, transfer to a roasting tin and roast in a preheated oven at 190°C (375°F) mark 5 for 20-25 minutes.

3 Meanwhile, for the sauce, melt the redcurrant jelly in the frying pan. Add the port and beef stock, and boil until reduced to a thick liquid. Add the cream and stir well. Season with salt and pepper to taste.

4 Take the lamb from the oven and slice into medallions. Pour the sauce on to warmed serving plates and fan the medallions of lamb out on top. Serve immediately.

FAN-ROASTED POTATOES

450 g (1 lb) potatoes
45-60 ml (3-4 tbsp) olive oil

1 Peel the potatoes and make evenly-spaced lengthwise cuts through them, leaving 1 cm (½ inch) intact at one end.

2 Heat the olive oil in a roasting tin, and when hot enough, put the potatoes in. Spoon the oil over the potatoes. Roast in a preheated oven at 190°C (375°F) mark 5 for 40-45 minutes until crisp and brown, basting every 20 minutes. Drain well and serve.

TARRAGON LEEKS

450 g (1 lb) leeks
50 g (2 oz) butter
bunch of tarragon leaves, stalks
  removed

1 Trim the leeks and cut into 5 cm (2 inch) lengths. Slice into strips, and wash thoroughly.

2 Melt the butter in a pan and add the tarragon leaves. Add the leek strips, put the lid on and continue cooking gently for 10 minutes.

3 Drain to serve.

GLAZED CARROTS

225 g (8 oz) small even-sized carrots
25 g (1 oz) caster sugar
25 g (1 oz) butter

1 Scrape the carrots and top and tail them. Place in a saucepan, just cover with water, and add the sugar and butter.

2 Bring to the boil, and boil rapidly for 10-12 minutes until the liquid has all but evaporated and the carrots are tender and glossy.

CHOCOLATE MOUSSE

50 g (2 oz) plain chocolate, in pieces
1 egg, separated
90 ml (3 fl oz) double cream
25 g (1 oz) hazelnuts, chopped

To Serve:
Biscuit Cups

1 Place the chocolate pieces in a heat-proof bowl over a pan of hot water and leave until melted. Stir until smooth.

2 Stir the egg yolk into the melted chocolate.

3 In a bowl, whip the cream until soft peaks form. Fold into the chocolate mixture, reserving a little for decoration.

4 Whisk the egg white until stiff, then fold into the chocolate mixture. Leave to thicken.

5 Spoon into biscuit cups and decorate with the reserved cream.

BISCUIT CUPS

25 g (1 oz) plain flour, sieved
50 g (2 oz) caster sugar
1 egg white
25 g (1 oz) butter
icing sugar, for dusting

1 Grease and flour a baking sheet.

2 Put the flour and sugar into a bowl, add the egg white and butter, and beat until smooth.

3 Spoon 10 ml (2 tsp) of mixture on to the prepared baking sheet and spread thinly into a round, using the back of a spoon. Repeat with the remaining mixture.

4 Bake in a preheated oven at 190°C (375°F) mark 5 for 5-7 minutes. Remove from the baking sheet using a thin spatula or fish slice and place individually over upturned dariole moulds to set into the shape of a cup. Leave until set, then carefully remove the biscuit cups.

5 To serve, dust with icing sugar.

SHAPING BISCUIT CUPS

Biscuits cups, made from wafer batter, are ideal crisp containers for serving mousses, ice creams and sorbets. If you haven't any dariole moulds, shape them over upturned tumblers. Should the biscuit rounds harden before you have time to mould them, return to the oven for a few moments to soften.

The North West

Contestants
Shabab Hashmie • Danielle Crowley • Sam Goss

Panel of Judges
**Antony Worrall-Thompson • Lee Chapman •
Loyd Grossman**

Sam Goss' Menu

MAIN COURSE

Harvester Steak with a Green Pepper Sauce

Wild Mushrooms

Warm Salad

"Quite a British product" **Antony Worrall-Thompson**

DESSERT

Celtic Red Fruit Compote, served with a Traditional Junket

"Very good combination of flavours" **Lee Chapman**

Thirteen year old Sam Goss comes from Port Soderick in the Isle of Man. Sam's home used to be the railway station, and during the summer months he travels to and from school by the old steam train which plies between Douglas and Port Erin. Sam's hobbies include rugby, shooting for pheasant in the nearby woods and fishing for Bollam Wrass from the rocky coastline.

Chicken Roulé with a Sun-dried Tomato and Mushroom Stuffing
HELEN DEACON'S MAIN COURSE (Regional Heat)

Hazelnut Meringue with White Chocolate Cream and a Raspberry Coulis
CAMILLA ASKAROFF'S DESSERT (Semi-Final)

Glazed Noisettes of Lamb with Apricot Stuffing
GRAHAM BOOTH'S MAIN COURSE (Semi Final)

Steamed Apricot Pudding with an Apricot and Pistachio Butterscotch Sauce
CAMILLA ASKAROFF'S DESSERT (Final)

HARVESTER STEAK WITH A GREEN PEPPER SAUCE

2 sirloin steaks, each about 175 g
    (6 oz)
75 g (3 oz) blue Stilton cheese,
    crumbled
1 small apple, peeled, cored and
    grated
finely chopped herbs (basil, thyme,
    oregano), to taste
salt and freshly ground black pepper
2 rashers back bacon
50 g (2 oz) whey butter (see below)

Sauce:
150-175 ml (5-6 fl oz) red wine
75 ml (5 tbsp) chicken or beef stock
pinch of grated fresh horseradish root
10 green peppercorns or juniper
    berries, crushed
150 ml (¼ pint) double cream or
    natural yogurt

1 With a sharp knife, make an incision lengthways in each steak and fill with the cheese and grated apple. Sprinkle with finely chopped fresh herbs, and season with salt and pepper.

2 Remove the rind from the bacon, and wrap a bacon rasher around each steak to hold the filling in place. Secure the opening with a wooden cocktail stick if necessary.

3 Melt the whey butter in a frying pan, add the steak parcels and cook each side for approximately 4 minutes. Remove and keep warm.

4 For the sauce, pour the red wine into the juices in the pan and simmer to reduce a little. Add the stock, grated horseradish and crushed peppercorns or juniper berries. Simmer for 2-3 minutes, then stir in the cream.

5 Serve the sauce either poured over the steaks or separately.

WHEY BUTTER

I have chosen to use whey butter because you can cook with it to a far higher temperature without it burning. Whey butter is available on the Isle of Man and in selected shops elsewhere. It is a by-product of cheese-making, made from the residue of cream in the whey drained from cheese curds. If you cannot obtain it, use clarified butter instead.

WILD MUSHROOMS

4-6 large flat wild field mushrooms
25-50 g (1-2 oz) whey butter
chopped parsley, to taste

1 Melt the whey butter in a frying pan, and add the mushrooms. Fry for about 2 minutes on each side.

2 Serve topped with the butter juices, and sprinkled with chopped parsley.

WARM SALAD

2 peppers (if possible, ½ each of red,
*   green, yellow and orange)*
6-8 cherry tomatoes
30 ml (2 tbsp) sesame oil
1 onion, chopped
2 small courgettes, chopped
salt and freshly ground black pepper
1 clove garlic, crushed
1 sprig of thyme, basil or oregano,
*   chopped*
15 ml (1 tbsp) white wine vinegar or
*   cider vinegar*

1 Remove the core and seeds from the peppers, then cut into slices. Skin the tomatoes, then chop them.

2 Heat the oil in a pan, add the onion and cook for 1 minute, then add the courgettes, peppers and tomatoes. Season, then add the garlic and herbs. Cook for 2-3 minutes; the vegetables should be crunchy.

3 Stir in the vinegar and serve warm.

CELTIC RED FRUIT COMPOTE

25 g (1 oz) raspberries
25 g (1 oz) redcurrants
25 g (1 oz) blackcurrants
50 g (2 oz) strawberries
25 g (1 oz) blackberries
25 g (1 oz) whortleberries or bilberries
75 g (3 oz) caster sugar
a little red wine (optional)
a little grated fresh root ginger
pinch of ground cinnamon
1 star anise
a little grated lemon rind

To Serve:
Traditional Junket

1 Prepare all the fruit, removing stalks etc. Set some aside for decoration.

2 Put the fruit into a heavy-based pan, sprinkle with the sugar and cover sparingly with water. Cook at a gentle heat for 3-4 minutes (don't overcook).

3 Remove half the fruit with a slotted spoon and set aside. Sieve the remaining fruit and juices through a nylon sieve and return to the pan. Add the wine if using, spices and lemon rind, and simmer until reduced and thickened. Taste and add more sugar if necessary.

4 Arrange the fruit in serving dishes, strain the fruit syrup over and decorate with the reserved fresh fruit.

COOK'S TIP

Remember – you can always add sugar to sweeten, but you can't take it away!

TRADITIONAL JUNKET

300 ml (½ pint) full-cream milk
5-10 ml (1-2 tsp) vanilla sugar (see below)
1 teaspoon rennet
freshly grated nutmeg

1 Pour the milk and sugar into a heavy-based saucepan and heat gently, stirring all the time until the sugar has dissolved and the mixture is at blood temperature.

2 Remove from the heat, add the rennet and stir in.

3 Pour into two individual glasses or serving dishes and top with freshly grated nutmeg. Leave aside to set. Do not move, or the junket will break into curds and whey.

VANILLA SUGAR

To make your own vanilla sugar, simple half-fill a screw-top jar with caster sugar. Put in a vanilla pod, and fill to the top with more caster sugar. Screw the lid on tightly. The sugar will absorb the vanilla flavour in a few days.

If you do not have any vanilla sugar to hand, use caster sugar and flavour the milk with a few drops of vanilla essence.

Contestants
Camilla Askaroff • Elizabeth Birch • Rebecca Jethwa

Panel of Judges
Darina Allen • Danny Baker • Loyd Grossman

WINNER

Camilla Askaroff's Menu

MAIN COURSE

Fillet of Arctic Char en Papillotte with Dill Hollandaise

Mustard Seed New Potatoes

Julienne of Fresh Vegetables

"Extraordinary fish" **Danny Baker**

DESSERT

Pear and Almond Tartlets with a Caramelised Topping, served
with Mascarpone Ice Cream

"That pastry was really exceptional" **Darina Allen**

"Irresistible" **Danny Baker**

Camilla Askaroff, who is 12 years old, lives in Herstmonceux in East Sussex. Camilla attends the Hailsham Community College where she participates in most sports. She's basketball captain and a stalwart member of the hockey team. Outside school, she enjoys cycling, with her mother and sister Natasha, who are also both enthusiastic cooks. In quieter moments, Camilla relaxes at home with her embroidery.

FILLET OF ARCTIC CHAR EN PAPILLOTE WITH DILL HOLLANDAISE

2 fillets of Arctic char, each about
175 g (6 oz)
½ lime, sliced
2 large fennel sprigs

Hollandaise Sauce:
15 ml (1 tbsp) white wine vinegar
freshly ground white pepper
125 g (4 oz) butter
1 egg yolk
15 ml (1 tbsp) chopped dill

To Garnish:
dill sprigs
lime slices

1 Skin the Arctic char fillets and place each one on a greased piece of foil. Top with the lime slices and fennel to flavour. Wrap the foil around the fish to enclose.

2 Cook in a preheated oven at 190°C (375°F) mark 5 for 15 minutes or until the fish is tender and flakes easily.

3 Meanwhile, make the sauce. Season the vinegar with pepper and bring to the boil in a small pan. At the same time, melt the butter until hot. Place the egg yolk in a bowl, add the hot vinegar and whisk together, then gradually add the hot butter and whisk until the mixture thickens. Add the chopped dill just before serving.

4 Remove the fish from the foil and place on warmed serving plates. Pour some hollandaise over the fish or to one side, and garnish with dill and a slice of lime. Serve at once.

ARCTIC CHAR

This fine-flavoured fish is a member of the salmon and trout family, most closely resembling the salmon trout. It has firm, sweet, pinkish-white flesh and is regarded as something of a delicacy. Most char weigh about 1 kg (2 lb).

MUSTARD SEED NEW POTATOES

about 225 g (8 oz) new potatoes
10 ml (2 tsp) coarse-grain mustard
15 ml (1 tbsp) walnut oil

1 Steam the new potatoes over boiling water until tender.

2 Mix the mustard and oil together in a bowl, then add the potatoes and toss well. Keep warm until ready to serve.

JULIENNE OF FRESH VEGETABLES

1 carrot
2 spring onions
2 chunks of cucumber, each about 5 cm (2 inch)
6 mangetouts
6 asparagus tips
15 g (½ oz) butter

1 Cut the carrot, spring onions and cucumber into julienne (matchstick strips).

2 Place all of the vegetables in a steamer and steam for about 30 seconds. Just before serving, melt the butter in a pan, add the vegetables and toss well over a medium heat to heat through and glaze.

PEAR AND ALMOND TARTLETS WITH A CARAMELISED TOPPING

Pastry:
75 g (3 oz) plain flour
25 g (1 oz) ground almonds
75 g (3 oz) butter, in pieces
7.5 ml (1½ tsp) icing sugar
about 30 ml (2 tbsp) cold water

Filling:
1 pear
150 ml (¼ pint) single cream
1 egg yolk
5 ml (1 tsp) vanilla extract

Caramelised Topping:
60 ml (4 tbsp) sugar
135 ml (9 tbsp) water
15 ml (1 tbsp) flaked almonds, toasted

To Serve:
Mascarpone Ice Cream (see right)
icing sugar, for dusting

1 To make the pastry, mix the flour and ground almonds together in a bowl. Add the butter and rub in until the mixture resembles fine crumbs. Stir in the icing sugar and enough water to form a soft dough. Wrap in cling film and chill in the refrigerator for 10 minutes.

2 Roll out the pastry on a lightly floured surface and use to line two greased 10 cm (4 inch) individual flan tins. Chill.

3 Peel, halve and core the pear, then cut into slices. Arrange half the pear slices in each pastry case. Mix together the cream, egg yolk and vanilla extract, and pour over the pear slices.

4 Bake the tartlets in a preheated oven at 190°C (375°F) mark 5 for 25 minutes until golden.

5 To make the caramelised topping, dissolve the sugar in the water in a heavy-based pan over a low heat, then increase the heat and cook, without stirring, to a golden brown caramel. Pour half of this over the cooked tartlets. Allow to cool.

6 Stir the toasted flaked almonds into the remaining caramel and pour on to a piece of greased foil. Leave to set – to make praline – and then crush into small pieces.

7 Serve the cooled tartlets on individual plates with scoops of Mascarpone Ice Cream. Sprinkle praline pieces over the ice cream, and dust the whole plate with sifted icing sugar.

MASCARPONE ICE CREAM

75 ml (5 tbsp) whipping cream
125 g (4 oz) mascarpone
10 ml (2 tsp) vanilla sugar

1 Mix all the ingredients together in a bowl until smooth. Place in an ice-cream maker and churn for about 10-15 minutes. Or place in a suitable container in the freezer until solid, whisking every now and again to break down the ice crystals and ensure smoothness.

Contestants
Camilla Askaroff • Elizabeth Birch • Rebecca Jethwa

Panel of Judges
Darina Allen • Danny Baker • Loyd Grossman

Elizabeth Birch's Menu

MAIN COURSE

Butterfly Lamb Steaks roasted over Rosemary, served
with Béarnaise Sauce

Crisp Green Vegetables

Dauphinois Potatoes

"Exceptionally good Dauphinois potatoes" **Loyd**

DESSERT

Pears Poached in Red wine, with Calvados-flavoured Cream

"Wonderful... a lovely, shiny, glossy sauce" **Darina Allen**

Fourteen year old Elizabeth Birch comes from Lymington in
Hampshire. Elizabeth is a keen rider, and enjoys nothing
more than a stiff canter through the surrounding New Forest on
her pony. Involved in the Duke of Edinburgh Award Scheme,
Elizabeth is doing her community service at the War Memorial
Hospital where her mother is an occupational therapist.
Back at Wentworth Milton Mount School, Elizabeth is a
leading light in the drama society's performance of
J.B. Priestley's *Mystery at Greenfingers*.

BUTTERFLY LAMB STEAKS ROASTED OVER ROSEMARY, SERVED WITH BÉARNAISE SAUCE

2 butterfly lamb steaks
about 30 ml (2 tbsp) olive oil
5 ml (1 tsp) finely chopped rosemary
salt and freshly ground black pepper
5 large rosemary sprigs

Béarnaise Sauce:
½ glass white wine
30 ml (2 tbsp) white wine vinegar
1 shallot, finely chopped
225 g (8 oz) butter
3 egg yolks

1 Trim off the fatty ends of the steaks. Season the olive oil with the finely chopped rosemary and salt and pepper, and brush the steaks with this.

2 Lie the sprigs of rosemary in the bottom of a roasting tin and place a rack over the top. Lie the lamb steaks on the rack (to allow the excess fat to drain away). Place in a preheated oven at 180°C (350°F) mark 4 for 30-40 minutes, or until cooked to your preference.

3 Meanwhile, make the béarnaise sauce. Put the wine, vinegar and shallot in a small saucepan and boil until reduced by half. Strain the liquid, discarding the shallot.

4 Melt the butter in a glass bowl, in the microwave. Allow to cool slightly, then add the egg yolks slowly, stirring all the time. Add the reduced wine and vinegar slowly, stirring constantly. Season with salt and pepper to taste.

5 Place in the microwave on high for 1½ minutes, stirring every 10 seconds. (If the sauce curdles, do not worry. Whisk briskly until it is 'repaired'!) The finished sauce should be thick and creamy.

6 To serve, pour the sauce on to warmed serving plates, and place the steaks on top.

COOK'S TIP

It is possible to make this béarnaise sauce in the traditional way but I find making it in the microwave is just as good, quicker and easier. For the traditional method, whisk the egg yolks and seasoning into the reduced wine vinegar mixture, then whisk over a low heat for about 4 minutes. Remove from the heat, and gradually whisk in the tepid butter until the sauce thickens.

DAUPHINOIS POTATOES

250 g (9 oz) potatoes
300 ml (½ pint) double cream
75 g (3 oz) Gruyère cheese, grated
freshly grated nutmeg, to taste

1 Peel and thinly slice the potatoes.

2 Heat the cream until beginning to boil.

3 In suitable ovenproof dishes, such as ramekins, layer the potatoes with the cheese and grated nutmeg until all the potato and cheese has been used.

4 Pour the cream over the potato in the dishes. Cook in a preheated oven at 180°C (350°F) mark 4 for 45 minutes. Serve in the dishes.

PEARS POACHED IN RED WINE WITH CALVADOS-FLAVOURED CREAM

2 small firm pears (see right)
100 g (3½ oz) sugar
75 ml (2½ fl oz) water
½ cinnamon stick
4 cloves
finely pared rind and juice of 1 orange
200 ml (7 fl oz) red wine (see right)
red food colouring (optional)

Cream:
150 ml (¼ pint) whipping cream
5 ml (1 tsp) Calvados (apple brandy)

1 Peel the pears and cut a thin slice off the bottoms so they can stand upright.

2 In a large saucepan combine the sugar, water, spices, orange rind and juice. Heat gently until the sugar has dissolved. Add the pears and simmer for 15 minutes.

3 Add the red wine, reserving 60 ml (4 tbsp), and cook over low heat for 15-30 minutes or until the pears are tender; test after 15 minutes.

4 When the pears are ready, take them out and place on serving dishes. Add the reserved wine to the pan and reduce the liquid to a light syrup. To enhance the colour if necessary, add a little red food colouring. Strain the syrup over the pears and chill.

5 For the cream, whip the cream until soft peaks form, then fold in the Calvados using a metal spoon. Serve separately.

COOK'S TIP

I have found William pears to be best in shape and texture for poaching. I usually use Corbières wine in this dish, as some other red wines turn the sauce brown.

REGIONAL HEATS
The South East

Contestants
Camilla Askaroff • Elizabeth Birch • Rebecca Jethwa

Panel of Judges
Darina Allen • Danny Baker • Loyd Grossman

Rebecca Jethwa's Menu

MAIN COURSE
Lamb and Cashew Nut Korma

Spiced Cauliflower Dhal

Pilau Rice

"Lovely taste sensation" **Darina Allen**

DESSERT
Lemon and Lime Drizzle Puddings

"Nice clean fresh taste" **Darina Allen**

Eleven-year-old Rebecca Jethwa comes from North Baddesley near Southampton and goes to the County Junior School. Rebecca is an extremely talented musician; she plays the piano, clarinet and recorder as well as her violin. The Jethwas' are a very 'green' family; they are all involved in regular surveys of the nearby coast, monitoring the litter and pollution levels of the Calshot beach. Like her brother Seth and sister Susanna, Rebecca enjoys disco dancing.

LAMB AND CASHEW NUT KORMA

2 boneless lamb leg steaks, cubed

Korma Sauce:
6 saffron threads
40 g (1½ oz) cashew nuts
2.5 cm (1 inch) fresh root ginger,
  peeled
1 cinnamon stick
6 cloves
2.5 ml (½ tsp) cardamom seeds
1.25 ml (¼ tsp) cumin seeds
1 chilli, halved and seeded
90 ml (3 fl oz) water
15 ml (1 tbsp) oil
1 onion, chopped
150 g (5 oz) plain yogurt
salt

To Garnish:
chopped coriander leaves
salad leaves

1 For the sauce, soak the saffron in 15 ml (1 tbsp) boiling water.

2 Put the cashew nuts, ginger, cinnamon stick, cloves, cardamom seeds, cumin seeds and chilli into a spice mill and grind to a powder (or use a pestle and mortar). Add the water and blend to a paste.

3 Heat the oil in a pan, and fry the onion until lightly browned. Add the spice mixture and yogurt, and heat through, stirring well.

Mix in the saffron and salt to taste.

4 Add the lamb and turn to coat with the sauce.

5 Bring to the boil, then reduce the heat and simmer, covered, for about 30 minutes.

6 Sprinkle with coriander and garnish with salad leaves to serve.

SPICED CAULIFLOWER DHAL

125 g (4 oz) dhal (yellow lentils)
15 ml (1 tbsp) oil
1 small onion, chopped
5 ml (1 tsp) ground cumin
5 ml (1 tsp) ground coriander
1.25 ml (¼ tsp) turmeric
1.25 ml (¼ tsp) chilli powder, or 1
  green chilli, seeded and chopped
1.25 ml (¼ tsp) freshly ground black
  pepper
salt
½ cauliflower, about 200 g (7 oz)

1 Wash the dhal and soak in enough cold water to cover for 1-2 hours. Drain well.

2 Heat the oil in a saucepan, add the onion and fry until lightly browned.

3 Mix the spices together, then add to the onion followed by the dhal. Simmer for about 30 minutes, until the dhal is beginning to soften, but is still retaining its shape. Season to taste with salt.

4 Cut the cauliflower into florets and add to the dhal mixture. Continue cooking until the cauliflower is tender, then serve.

DHAL

Dhal is the general Hindi name for lentils and other split pulses. Yellow and red lentils are both used in Indian cooking.

PILAU RICE

125 g (4 oz) basmati rice
15 ml (1 tbsp) oil
1 potato, peeled and cubed
1.25 ml (¼ tsp) mustard seeds
1.25 ml (¼ tsp) cumin seeds
300 ml (½ pint) water
5 cm (2 inch) cinnamon stick
2 cloves
1.25 ml (¼ tsp) turmeric
50 g (2 oz) shelled peas
salt to taste

1 Wash the rice and soak in enough cold water to cover for about 15-20 minutes.

2 Heat the oil in a saucepan, add the potato with the mustard and cumin seeds and fry until the potato cubes begin to brown.

3 Drain the rice and add to the potato with the measured water, the cinnamon stick, cloves, turmeric and peas. Put the lid on the pan and bring to the boil, then reduce the heat. Replace the lid and leave to simmer for about 20-25 minutes.

4 Take out the cinnamon stick and cloves, and serve.

LEMON AND LIME DRIZZLE PUDDINGS

150 ml (¼ pint) double cream
1 lime
1 lemon
45 ml (3 tbsp) icing sugar

Sponge:
50 g (2 oz) butter
75 g (3 oz) caster sugar
75 g (3 oz) plain flour
5 ml (1 tsp) baking powder
22.5 ml (1½ tbsp) milk
1 egg

To Serve:
1 lime and 1 lemon, sliced

1 In a bowl, whip the cream until thick, then put it in the refrigerator.

2 Grate the rind from the lemon and lime, and squeeze the juices into a bowl.

3 Make the sponge. Cream the butter and sugar together in a bowl, then add the flour, baking powder, milk, egg and three quarters of the grated lemon and lime rind. Beat together thoroughly.

4 Grease and line 4 individual flan tins with greaseproof paper, and divide the sponge mixture between them. Bake in a preheated oven at 190°C (375°F) mark 5 for 20 minutes. Remove from the oven.

5 To make the drizzle, heat the lemon and lime juices with the icing sugar.

6 Prick the sponges with a fork then pour the drizzle on each sponge. Leave to cool.

7 To serve, remove the sponges from their tins and take off the greaseproof paper. Serve decorated with the whipped cream and remaining grated citrus rind. Surround with lemon and lime slices.

Note: This recipe makes 4 puddings.

The First Semi-Final

Contestants
Camilla Askaroff • Yoav Preiss • Nicola Trundle

Panel of Judges
Shaun Hill • Kika Mirylees • Loyd Grossman

WINNER

Camilla Askaroff's Menu

MAIN COURSE

Fillet of Beef on a bed of Oyster Mushrooms and Spiced
Vegetables

Parsnip Bake

"An excellent idea" **Shaun Hill**

Fresh Tomato Pasta

DESSERT

Hazelnut Meringues with White Chocolate Cream Filling and a
Raspberry Coulis

"Slightly chewy inside, crisp on the outside – perfect" **Shaun Hill**

"An amazing meringue" **Loyd**

FILLET OF BEEF ON A BED OF OYSTER MUSHROOMS AND SPICED VEGETABLES

350 g (12 oz) piece of beef fillet
freshly ground black pepper
60 ml (4 tbsp) olive oil
2 spring onions, sliced into rings
1 clove garlic, crushed
5 ml (1 tsp) freshly grated root ginger
½ lemon grass stalk, bruised and finely
  chopped
1.25 ml (¼ tsp) ground coriander
½ red pepper, cored, seeded and thinly
  sliced
1 small red chilli, seeded and shredded
125 g (4 oz) oyster mushrooms
60 ml (4 tbsp) white wine
2.5 ml (½ tsp) arrowroot
5 ml (1 tsp) honey
coarsely chopped coriander leaves, to
  taste

1 Season the beef generously with pepper. Heat 30 ml (2 tbsp) olive oil in a roasting tin on the hob, add the beef and seal on all sides over a high heat. Transfer to a preheated oven at 200°C (400°F) mark 6 and roast for 23 minutes; this gives medium rare meat.

2 About 5 minutes before the meat will be ready, heat 30 ml (2 tbsp) olive oil in a frying pan. Add the spring onions, garlic, ginger, lemon grass and coriander; fry, stirring, for about 1 minute. Then add the red pepper, chilli and mushrooms; cook for a further 2-3 minutes.

3 In a cup, mix the white wine with the arrowroot and honey, then add to the vegetables with the meat juices from the roasting tin. Cook gently, stirring, until thickened. Stir in some chopped coriander to taste just before serving.

4 Slice the meat carefully into about 6 thick slices. Spoon the vegetables onto warmed serving plates and arrange the meat on top. Drizzle some of the sauce over the meat. Serve with the fresh tomato pasta and parsnip bake.

FRESH TOMATO PASTA

1 egg (size 3)
100 g (3½ oz) plain flour
15 ml (1 tbsp) tomato purée
pinch of salt

1 Put all the ingredients in a food processor and work until a smooth dough is formed. Place in a plastic bag and set aside for 10-15 minutes to rest.

2 Flour the pasta lightly and put through a pasta machine on the widest setting. Repeat, reducing the setting by one notch each time, until you reach thickness 5, then put through the tagliatelle cutters. Hang over a clean pole or drape on a clean tea towel and leave for 5-10 minutes to dry. (Alternatively if you haven't got a pasta machine roll the dough out thinly on a lightly floured surface and cut into ribbons of tagliatelle.)

3 Cook in a large pan of boiling salted water for 2-3 minutes until *al dente* (tender but firm to the bite). Drain thoroughly and serve.

PARSNIP BAKE

1 parsnip, peeled and cubed
¼ onion, chopped
40 g (1½ oz) butter
about 120 ml (4 fl oz) chicken stock
1 slice brown bread, crusts removed
1.25 ml (¼ tsp) paprika
2.5 ml (½ tsp) dry mustard
30 ml (2 tbsp) soured cream
freshly ground black pepper
pinch of chilli powder

1 Place the parsnip and onion in a saucepan with 25 g (1 oz) butter over a medium heat. When the butter is sizzling, add enough stock to cover the parsnip, then simmer for 20 minutes. Drain.

2 Meanwhile whizz the bread in a food processor or blender to make breadcrumbs.

3 Mix the parsnips and onion with the paprika and dry mustard, then add the soured cream. Stir well and add a good grind of black pepper.

4 Divide the parsnip mixture between 2 small ramekins and top with the breadcrumbs and 3 tiny knobs of butter per ramekin. Place in the top of a preheated oven at 180°C (350°F) mark 4 for 10 minutes or until the breadcrumbs begin to crisp and brown.

5 Serve in the ramekins, sprinkled with a little chilli powder.

HAZELNUT MERINGUES WITH A WHITE CHOCOLATE CREAM FILLING AND A RASPBERRY COULIS

1 egg white
50 g (2 oz) vanilla sugar
25 g (1 oz) toasted hazelnuts, coarsely
  ground
1.25 ml (¼ tsp) white wine vinegar

Filling:
75 g (3 oz) white chocolate, broken into
  pieces
150 ml (¼ pint) double cream

Coulis:
225 g (8 oz) raspberries
10 ml (2 tsp) icing sugar

To Decorate:
icing sugar, for dusting
a little single cream
dark chocolate curls (see below)
few raspberries

1 Preheat the oven to 180°C (350°F) mark 4; grease four 10 cm (4 inch) individual flan tins and line with non-stick baking parchment.

2 For the meringue, whisk the egg white until stiff, then whisk in the sugar 15 ml (1 tbsp) at a time. Fold in the ground hazelnuts and vinegar. Spoon the meringue into the prepared tins and cook in the preheated oven for 20-25 minutes. Leave to cool, then carefully remove from the tins. Remove the paper.

3 Meanwhile, make the filling. Melt the chocolate in a bowl over a pan of hot water. Whisk the double cream until stiff, then fold in the melted chocolate. Place in the refrigerator.

4 For the coulis, put the raspberries and icing sugar in the food processor, and blend until smooth. Sieve to get rid of the seeds.

5 Divide the raspberry coulis between the 2 individual serving plates. Put one of the meringue rounds on each plate. Cover with the filling. Put another meringue round on top and dust with icing sugar. Decorate the meringues with chocolate curls. Dot the raspberry coulis with single cream and feather with a skewer. Place a few raspberries in the coulis. Serve at once.

CHOCOLATE CURLS

To make simple chocolate curls, use a vegetable peeler to shave curls from the side of a block of chocolate. The chocolate should be at cool room temperature.

──The First Semi-Final──

Contestants
Camilla Askaroff • Yoav Preiss • Nicola Trundle

Panel of Judges
Shaun Hill • Kika Mirylees • Loyd Grossman

Yoav Preiss' Menu

MAIN COURSE
Duck with Fennel Sauce
"Tender and delicious" **Kika Mirylees**
Polenta
Givetch (Romanian Vegetable Dish)

DESSERT
Mango Mousse with Kiwi and Passion Fruit
"Sharp and tangy" **Kika Mirylees**

DUCK WITH FENNEL SAUCE

1 small duck, 1-1.3 kg (2-3 lb), cleaned
30 ml (2 tbsp) grated fresh root ginger
60 ml (4 tbsp) soy sauce
1 fennel bulb, sliced
45 ml (3 tbsp) sherry
250 ml (8 fl oz) chicken stock
45 ml (3 tbsp) brown sugar
juice of 1 large orange
7.5 ml (1½ tsp) cornflour
oil for deep-frying

To Serve:
polenta
chicken stock

1 Prick the duck all over with a sharp knife. Rub with 15 ml (1 tbsp) each of the ginger and soy sauce. Place the remaining ginger inside the duck, along with a large slice of the fennel.

2 Cut the rest of the fennel into smaller pieces. Place the remaining soy sauce, fennel, sherry, stock and sugar in a bowl.

3 Place the duck, breast up, in a saucepan large enough to hold it. Pour in the soy mixture, cover and cook over a medium heat for 40-50 minutes, turning the duck every 10 minutes.

4 Meanwhile, make the polenta. Follow the packet instructions, using chicken stock instead of water. Cook until thick, then pour on to a plate and allow to 'set'. Cut into the desired shapes. Warm through in the oven to serve.

5 Remove the duck from the pan and cut in half along the breastbone. Keep warm.

6 Place all the cooking liquor and fennel in a blender or food processor, add the orange juice and blend to a purée. (Or push through a sieve.) Return to the cleaned pan. Mix the cornflour with a little water and add to the sauce. Cook, stirring constantly, over a low heat for 1-2 minutes, until thickened and smooth.

7 Heat the oil for deep-frying in a deep-fryer. When hot deep-fry the duck, one half at a time, until brown and crisp. Drain well.

8 Carve the duck breasts into slices. Serve, fanned out on warmed serving plates, with the polenta, givetch (see overleaf) and fennel sauce.

GIVETCH

1 red pepper
1 green pepper
1 yellow pepper
1 onion
1 small aubergine
2 small courgettes
oil for deep-frying

Sauce:
½ x 400 g (14 oz) tin chopped
   tomatoes with herbs
7.5 ml (½ tbsp) chopped parsley
2.5-5 ml (1-2 tsp) thyme leaves
4 basil leaves
15 ml (1 tbsp) tomato purée
10 ml (2 tsp) sugar
1 clove garlic, crushed
15 ml (1 tbsp) balsamic vinegar
7.5 ml (½ tbsp) soy sauce
juice of ½ lemon
salt and freshly ground black pepper

1 Halve the peppers crosswise, remove the core and seeds, then slice into rings. Slice the onion, aubergine and courgettes into rounds.

2 Heat the oil in a deep-fryer. When hot, deep-fry the vegetables in batches until soft and slightly brown, but not crisp. Drain thoroughly on kitchen paper.

3 For the sauce, combine all the ingredients in a bowl.

4 Put the warm vegetables in a dish, pour on the cold sauce and toss carefully to mix. Serve warm.

MANGO MOUSSE WITH KIWI AND PASSION FRUIT

juice of 1 lemon
30 ml (2 tbsp) water
1 sachet powdered gelatine
5 eggs
75 g (3 oz) caster sugar
175 g (6 oz) fresh mango pulp
250 ml (8 fl oz) whipping cream

To Serve:
2 kiwi fruit
2 passion fruit
*grapes and orange segments, to
   decorate*

1 Put the lemon juice and water in a small heatproof bowl, sprinkle on the gelatine and leave to one side for 5 minutes.

2 Whisk the eggs and sugar together, using an electric beater, until creamy and fluffy.

3 Stand the bowl of softened gelatine over a pan of simmering water until it dissolves. Allow to cool a little.

4 Add the mango pulp to the egg mixture a little at a time, whisking constantly, then beat in the gelatine gradually.

5 In a separate bowl, whip the cream until thick, then fold into the mousse until evenly incorporated.

6 Spoon the mousse mixture into individual moulds or cups, and chill in the refrigerator until set.

7 Peel the kiwi fruit and purée them in a blender or food processor. Halve the passion fruit, scoop out the pulp and seeds and add to the kiwi. Divide between the serving plates. Turn out the mango mousses on top of the coulis and decorate with grapes and orange segments to serve.

PREPARING MANGO PULP

Make sure you choose a ripe, juicy, flavourful mango, which will 'give' if gently squeezed. Remove the peel, using a vegetable peeler, then slice the flesh away from the large central stone. Purée in a blender or food processor until smooth.

The First Semi-Final

Nicola Trundle's Menu

MAIN COURSE

Loin of Lamb with Chestnut Mushroom Moulds

DESSERT

Rich Apricot Cream

LOIN OF LAMB WITH CHESTNUT MUSHROOM MOULDS

350 g (12 oz) loin of lamb
salt and freshly ground black pepper
few thyme sprigs
about 30 ml (2 tbsp) oil

Mushroom Moulds:
65 g (2½ oz) chestnut mushrooms
100 g (3½ oz) butter
2 French beans, halved lengthwise
1 small carrot, sliced and briefly cooked
100 g (3½ oz) shallots, chopped
2 egg whites
125 g (4 oz) skinless chicken breast
  fillet, roughly chopped
30 ml (2 tbsp) crème fraîche

Sauce:
1 shallot, chopped
40 g (1½ oz) butter
140 g (4½ oz) chestnut mushrooms,
  chopped
150 ml (¼ pint) port
175 ml (6 fl oz) crème fraîche

1 Start by making the mushroom moulds. Use 10 ml (2 tsp) butter to grease 2 ramekins well. Put a cross of French beans with thin slices of cooked carrot between in the bottom of each.

2 Fry the shallots in half the remaining butter until golden. Fry the mushrooms in the rest of the butter until lightly cooked.

3 Put the shallots and mushrooms into a food processor, then add the egg whites, chicken breast and crème fraîche. Work until smooth.

4 Spoon this paste into the ramekins on top of the vegetable decoration. Stand the ramekins in a bain-marie or roasting tin containing enough hot water to come halfway up the sides. Cook in a preheated oven at 180°C (350°F) mark 4 for 15 minutes.

5 Season the lamb with salt and press the thyme sprigs into the meat. Heat the oil in a frying pan, add the lamb and brown on all sides. Transfer to the oven and roast for 10 minutes.

6 Meanwhile for the sauce, fry the shallot in the butter until soft, then add the chopped mushrooms and sauté for 1 minute. Add the port, crème fraîche and salt and pepper to taste. Simmer to reduce.

7 To serve, slice the lamb and arrange on warmed serving plates. Turn out the mushroom moulds beside the lamb. Pour the sauce around and serve at once.

RICH APRICOT CREAM

*160 g (5½ oz) ready-to-eat dried
  apricots*
juice of ⅓ lemon
45 ml (3 tbsp) brandy
1 egg white
185 ml (6½ fl oz) double cream

To Decorate:
a little whipped cream
grated plain chocolate

1 Put the apricots into a pan and just cover with water. Bring to the boil, lower the heat and simmer for 25 minutes. Drain.

2 Put the apricots, lemon juice and brandy in a food processor or blender and work to a purée.

3 Whisk the egg white until firm peaks form. In a separate bowl whip the cream until thick. Fold both the egg white and cream into the apricot purée. Divide the mixture between 2 ramekins.

4 Chill before serving, decorated with whipped cream and grated chocolate. Accompany with crisp dessert biscuits if you like.

DRIED APRICOTS

Some types of dried apricots are specially tenderised so that there is no need to soak them before use. Use this kind for the above recipe.

———— The Second Semi-Final ————

Contestants
Katie Targett-Adams • Shabab Hashmie • Katy Savage

Panel of Judges
Caroline Waldegrave • Andi Peters • Loyd Grossman

WINNER

Katie Targett-Adams' Menu

MAIN COURSE

Tricolore Lattice of Scottish Salmon, Sole and Spinach in a Puff
Pastry Box

Broccoli and Cauliflower Timbales with a Crunchy Almond Topping

Peppers, Cucumbers and Olives in a Warm Vinaigrette

"Perfectly seasoned, perfectly cooked" **Caroline Waldegrave**

DESSERT

Bitter Chocolate Truffle Pudding

"Just stunning, absolutely brilliant" **Caroline Waldegrave**

TRICOLORE LATTICE OF SCOTTISH SALMON, SOLE AND SPINACH IN A PUFF PASTRY BOX

Pastry:
75 g (3 oz) butter
125 g (4 oz) plain flour
pinch of salt
45-60 ml (3-4 tbsp) cold water, to mix
1 egg, beaten

Fish lattices:
225 g (8 oz) tail piece of salmon,
  skinned and boned
225 g (8 oz) fillet of sole, skinned
handful of spinach leaves
salt and freshly ground white pepper
25 g (1 oz) butter

1 For the pastry, wrap the measured butter in foil and place in the freezer for 30-45 minutes. Meanwhile sift the flour and salt into a mixing bowl.

2 Take the butter from the freezer and, holding it in the foil, dip into the flour, then grate it into the flour. Keep on dipping the fat into the flour to make it easier to grate. Distribute the butter evenly with a palette knife, and add enough water to form a dough that leaves the sides of the bowl clean, using your hands to bring it together. Put the dough into a polythene bag and chill in the refrigerator for 30 minutes.

3 Roll out the pastry on a floured board to a 5 mm (¼ inch) thickness. Cut into 12 strips, about 8 cm (3½ inches) long and 2 cm (¾ inch) wide. (You need to have some left for the bases). Space 3 strips a little apart and parallel on the work surface. Weave another 3 strips through these to make a lattice. Then repeat the process with the remaining 6 strips to make a second lattice.

4 Roll out the remaining pastry and cut two 8 cm (3½ inch) square bases. Transfer all 4 pieces of pastry to a greased baking tray, brush with the beaten egg and chill in the refrigerator.

5 Cut the salmon into 6 strips, 8 cm (3½ inches) long and 3 cm (1¼ inch) wide; repeat with the sole. Lay 3 salmon strips vertically and weave 3 sole strips through (in the same way as the pastry) to make a lattice pattern.

6 Bring a pan of water to the boil, add the spinach and blanch for 1 minute. Drain and rinse the spinach under cold running water to refresh. Roll 3 long pieces of spinach and place diagonally over the fish. Repeat with the second fish lattice. Season with salt and pepper.

7 Trim the edges of the fish lattices to form neat squares to fit on top of the pastry bases. Place small knobs of butter randomly on the fish lattices and, using a fish slice, transfer each to a piece of foil which is large enough to make a parcel. Place the fish parcels on a baking tray and bake along with the pastry lattices in a preheated oven at 180°C (350°F) mark 4 for 15-20 minutes, or until the pastry is golden brown and the fish is tender.

8 To serve, place the pastry bases to one side of each warmed serving plate and arrange the fish lattices on top. Put the pastry lattices on top at an angle. Serve with the accompaniments (see right).

COOK'S TIP

Any varieties of fish can be used for the tricolore lattice but it looks particularly effective with fish which have contrasting coloured flesh.

BROCCOLI AND CAULIFLOWER TIMBALES WITH A CRUNCHY ALMOND TOPPING

1 small head of broccoli
1 small cauliflower
salt and freshly ground black pepper
10 young spinach leaves, blanched

Mustard Sauce:
25 g (1 oz) butter
25 g (1 oz) plain flour
175 ml (6 fl oz) milk
15 ml (1 tbsp) wholegrain mustard

Almond Topping:
25 g (1 oz) fresh breadcrumbs
25 g (1 oz) butter
20 g (¾ oz) blanched almonds, finely
  chopped

1 Bring a large saucepan of salted water to the boil. Divide the broccoli and cauliflower into small florets and add to the pan. Boil for 3-4 minutes until just tender. Drain and leave to cool.

2 To make the mustard sauce, melt the butter in a pan, stir in the flour and cook for 2-3 minutes, stirring until the sauce begins to bubble and leave the sides of the pan. Add the milk gradually, then bring to the boil, stirring all the time. Cook for 1-2 minutes. Season with salt and pepper, then stir in the mustard.

3 Grease 2 heatproof bowls, about 10 cm (4 inches) wide and 6 cm (2½ inches) deep. Pack the broccoli and cauliflower alternately around the bowl. Pour 15 ml (1 tbsp) of mustard sauce into the middle and top with more broccoli and cauli-flower. Cover with foil and put a weight on top. Leave for 30 minutes. Bake in a preheated oven at 180°C (350°F) mark 4 for 10-15 minutes until heated through.

4 Meanwhile make the topping. Melt the butter in a frying pan and add the almonds and breadcrumbs. Cook gently for 3-4 minutes until browned.

5 To serve, arrange the spinach on the warmed plates and invert the timbales on top. Sprinkle with the topping.

PEPPERS, CUCUMBER AND OLIVES IN A WARM VINAIGRETTE

1 small yellow pepper
1 small red pepper
5 or 6 black pitted olives, halved
½ cucumber

Vinaigrette:
60 ml (2 fl oz) raspberry vinegar
5 ml (1 tsp) Dijon mustard
1 shallot, finely chopped
5 ml (1 tsp) thin honey
salt and freshly ground black pepper
30 ml (2 tbsp) virgin olive oil

1 For the vinaigrette, whisk together the raspberry vinegar, mustard, chopped shallot, honey and seasoning. Add the olive oil, whisking constantly, until the vinaigrette is well emulsified. Or put the ingredients in a screw-topped jar and shake well to combine.

2 Quarter, core and deseed the peppers; cut the cucumber into thin slices. Using small star cutters, cut out 2 small stars from each vegetable and the olives, then cut 2 stars from each with a larger star cutter.

3 To serve, place the vinaigrette in a pan and heat until warmed through; do not boil. Spoon onto the serving plates with the tricolore lattice and sprinkle the star vegetables around each plate.

BITTER CHOCOLATE TRUFFLE PUDDING

*150 g (5 oz) good-quality dark
    chocolate*
50 g (2 oz) unsalted butter
1 egg, separated
30 ml (2 tbsp) Grand Marnier
30 ml (2 tbsp) water
6 boudoir biscuits (savoiadi)
2 strips stripey sponge (see right)

To Decorate:
1 orange
cocoa powder, for dusting

1 Melt the chocolate in a heatproof bowl over a saucepan of hot water. Add a drop of water and a knob of butter to the chocolate and keep stirring. Cream the remaining butter until soft and add to the melted mixture.

2 Take the chocolate off the heat and stir in the beaten egg yolk, Grand Marnier and water. Crush the boudoir biscuits and add to the mixture. Beat the egg white until stiff, and gently fold into the chocolate mixture.

3 Line two 7.5 cm (3 inch) diameter metal rings, 6 cm (2½ inches) high (similar to a biscuit cutter but higher) with stripey sponge; place on a small baking tray. Fill with the chocolate mixture and place in the freezer for 30 minutes, then in the refrigerator for 30 minutes.

4 Peel the orange as though peeling an apple to remove all white pith, then with a sharp knife cut out the segments.

5 When the puddings have set, sprinkle the tops with sifted cocoa. Dip a tea towel in boiling water and rub around the outside of the rings to loosen the chocolate puddings. Slide out of the rings on to individual serving plates.

6 Covering half of the plate with a piece of paper, sift cocoa on to the other half. Arrange the orange segments around the pudding.

STRIPEY SPONGE

2 whole eggs, separated
1 egg yolk
40 g (1½ oz) caster sugar
45 g (1¾ oz) plain flour, sifted
10 ml (2 tsp) cocoa powder, sifted

1 Put all 3 egg yolks in a bowl with two thirds of the sugar and beat thoroughly until well amalgamated.

2 In another bowl, whisk the egg whites until stiff, add the remaining sugar and beat again for 1 minute. Fold one third into the yolk mixture until evenly incorporated. Add the remaining whites and fold gently into the mixture. Sprinkle the flour over the mixture and gently fold in.

3 Divide the mixture in half and place in separate bowls. Add the cocoa to one half and gently fold it in.

4 Preheat the oven to 220°C (425°F) mark 7. Line the base of a Swiss roll tin with greased greaseproof paper.

5 Put the two mixtures into piping bags, each fitted with a small nozzle. Starting with the plain mixture, pipe diagonal lines across the Swiss roll tin, leaving an equal space between each line. Pipe the chocolate mixture in between to fill the spaces.

6 Place in the preheated oven for about 5-6 minutes until just firm to the touch. When cooked tip out on to a sheet of greaseproof paper. Cut into strips when cool.

──The Second Semi-Final──

Contestants
Katie Targett-Adams • Shabab Hashmie • Katy Savage

Panel of Judges
Caroline Waldegrave • Andi Peters • Loyd Grossman

Shabab Hashmie's Menu

MAIN COURSE
Meat Korma

Biryani

"It tasted beautiful" **Andi Peters**
"I love the fresh clean taste... and the spices" **Loyd**

DESSERT
Halva

MEAT KORMA

450 g (1 lb) lamb chops
40 ml (2½ tbsp) clarified butter
1 onion, chopped
5 ml (1 tsp) chilli powder
5 ml (1 tsp) ground coriander
5 ml (1 tsp) ground ginger
salt and freshly ground black pepper
4 cloves garlic, crushed
45 ml (3 tbsp) natural yogurt
1 medium tomato, roughly chopped
500 ml (16 fl oz) water

To Serve:
Biryani (see right)
chopped coriander leaves, to taste

1 Heat the clarified butter in a frying pan, add the chopped onion and fry until softened and browned. Remove from the pan with a slotted spoon and set aside.

2 To the butter remaining in the pan, add the spices, 5 ml (1 tsp) salt, the garlic, natural yogurt and tomato. Stir well, then add the lamb chops, turning to coat in the spice mixture. Cook very gently for 15-20 minutes.

3 Increase the heat and stir for 3-4 minutes. Turn the heat down again, add the water and simmer gently for a further 15-20 minutes.

4 Serve the korma on top of the biryani (see right), sprinkled with coriander leaves and pepper to taste.

BIRYANI

450 g (1 lb) basmati rice
30 ml (2 tbsp) clarified butter
salt
orange food colouring

Stock:
450 g (1 lb) lamb chops
1 cinnamon stick
2 cloves
1 black and 1 green cardamom
1 onion, quartered

1 Wash the rice well in a sieve under cold running water, then leave to soak in a bowl of cold water for about 20 minutes.

2 Meanwhile, make the stock. Put all the ingredients in a pan and add enough water to cover them. Cover with a lid, bring to the boil, then leave to simmer for 20-25 minutes.

3 Strain the stock, keeping the meat, but discarding the onion and spices. Remove the meat from the bones and cut into smaller pieces.

4 Drain the rice very well.

5 Heat the clarified butter in a pan, add the reserved meat and fry for 2-3 minutes, then add the rice and stock, making sure there is enough stock to cover the rice by 1 cm (½ inch). Season with a pinch of salt and leave to cook gently until the rice has absorbed all the liquid.

6 Place a tiny blob of orange food colouring at the edge of the rice, a little in from the side of the pan. Put a tea towel on top of the pan, taking care the ends do not trail near the heat, and top with the lid. Leave to gently steam and cook for a further 2-4 minutes.

7 Fluff up the rice when ready to serve, to roughly distribute the orange colour. Serve hot.

CLARIFIED BUTTER

This can be heated to a higher temperature than ordinary butter without burning. To prepare, melt butter in a pan over a low heat, then skim the froth from the surface. Remove from the heat and allow to stand until the sediment settles on the bottom of the pan. Carefully pour the clarified butter into a bowl, leaving the sediment behind.

HALVA

175 g (6 oz) caster sugar
400 ml (14 fl oz) water
225 g (8 oz) semolina
2 green cardamom pods, split
125 g (4 oz) butter
roughly chopped almonds, to decorate
  (optional)

1 Put the caster sugar and water in a saucepan and dissolve over a low heat, then bring to the boil.

2 In another saucepan, put the semolina and seeds from the cardamom pods. Stir over a medium heat until the semolina turns a green colour. Add the butter and cook, stirring, for another 2-3 minutes.

3 Add the sugar syrup to the semolina and continue to stir over a low heat until the halva thickens.

4 Serve hot or cold, sprinkled with chopped almonds if you wish.

──── The Second Semi-Final ────

Contestants
Katie Targett-Adams • Shabab Hashmie • Katy Savage

Panel of Judges
Caroline Waldegrave • Andi Peters • Loyd Grossman

Katy Savage's Menu

MAIN COURSE
Beef in Brown Ale

Red Cabbage

Pan Haggerty

"The Haggerty was innovative... wonderful" **Andi Peters**

DESSERT
Jamaican Lime Surprise

"A wonderful pudding" **Loyd**

───────

BEEF IN BROWN ALE

450 g (1 lb) braising beef, cut into
    large chunks
25 g (1 oz) butter
15 ml (1 tbsp) olive oil
1 onion, roughly chopped
plain flour, for coating
salt and freshly ground black pepper
a little extra Newcastle Brown Ale

Marinade:
¾ bottle Newcastle Brown Ale
1 thyme sprig
finely pared rind of 1 orange

Croûtons:
2 slices bread
about 25 g (1 oz) butter
about 10 ml (2 tsp) wholegrain mustard

To Garnish:
chopped parsley

1 Put the beef in a shallow dish and add the marinade ingredients. Stir well, cover and leave to marinate for 24 hours.

2 Preheat the oven to 190°C (375°F) mark 5, and put a casserole dish (preferably earthenware) in it to warm through.

3 Heat the butter and olive oil together in a large frying pan. Add the onion and fry gently until golden. Remove from the pan with a slotted spoon and keep to one side.

4 Remove the meat from the marinade, using a slotted spoon, and pat dry with kitchen paper. Toss in the flour to coat evenly. Heat the fat remaining in the frying pan and seal the meat in batches, 2 or 3 pieces at a time, until light brown in colour on all sides.

5 Return all the meat and onion to the frying pan, add the marinade and bring to the boil. Transfer to the warm casserole dish and season with salt and pepper. Place in the preheated oven and cook for about 1½ hours.

6 About 30 minutes before the meat will be ready, prepare the croûtons. Spread the bread with butter on one side, and with mustard on the other. Cut into large chunks.

7 About 20 minutes before the meat is ready, put the croûtons on top of the meat, butter side down.

8 About 10 minutes before you serve the stew, add a little more brown ale to it, to bring out the flavour.

9 Serve the stew sprinkled with chopped parsley, and accompanied by the red cabbage and Pan Haggerty.

RED CABBAGE

¼ red cabbage, thinly shedded
1 eating apple, peeled, cored and
  sliced
15 ml (1 tbsp) olive oil
6 cloves
5 ml (1 tsp) ground mixed spice
5 ml (1 tsp) demerara sugar
dash of red wine vinegar

1 Put the shredded cabbage and the apple in a pan with the olive oil. Add the cloves, mixed spice, sugar, vinegar and a splash of boiling water. Bring to the boil.

2 Cover and simmer over a low heat for about 20-30 minutes, stirring occasionally.

COOK'S TIP

The easiest way to shred the red cabbage is to use the food processor and shredder disc.

PAN HAGGERTY

about 25 g (1 oz) beef dripping
3 potatoes, peeled and thinly sliced
1 onion, thinly sliced
salt and freshly ground black pepper

1 Melt the dripping in a small frying pan, then take the pan off the heat.

2 Put a layer of potato slices on the bottom of the pan, then a layer of onions. Season well with salt and pepper. Continue layering in the same way until all the ingredients are used, finishing with a top layer of potatoes.

3 Cover the frying pan with foil and put it back on a very, very low heat, for about 20 minutes.

4 Take off the foil and put the pan under a preheated grill to brown the top. Serve hot, cut in wedges.

COOK'S TIP

For best results, use the thin slicing disc of the food processor to slice the potatoes.

JAMAICAN LIME SURPRISE

25 g (1 oz) butter
125 g (4 oz) caster sugar
juice and grated rind of 2 small limes
2 eggs, separated
90 ml (3 fl oz) milk
25 g (1 oz) rum
25 g (1 oz) plain flour, sifted
icing sugar, for dusting

1 Cream together the butter and 30 ml (2 tbsp) of the sugar with an electric hand mixer. Stir in the lime juice and rind.

2 Put the egg yolks in a bowl and beat in the milk and rum. Add this, little by little, to the creamed mixture, alternately with the flour and remaining sugar. Beat until the mixture is thoroughly blended.

3 Whisk the egg whites until stiff, but not dry. Fold them into the mixture with a metal spoon.

4 Grease 4 ramekins with butter and divide the mixture between them. Stand the ramekins in a roasting tin and pour boiling water into the tin to come halfway up the sides of the dishes. Bake in a preheated oven at 190°C (375°F) mark 5 for about 25 minutes until risen.

5 Serve straight from the oven, dusted with icing sugar. The puddings should turn out light and spongy on the top, with a tangy lime sauce hidden underneath.

Note: This recipe makes 4.

──── The Third Semi-Final ────

Contestants
Miranda Tetley • Graham Booth • Gaia Skibinski

Panel of Judges
Alastair Little • Janet Street-Porter • Loyd Grossman

WINNER

Miranda Tetley's Menu

MAIN COURSE
Pork Fillet in Rich Onion and Madeira Sauce
Small Roast Potatoes with Thyme
Baked Carrots
Spinach Nests with Mushrooms and Bacon in Cream
"I do like extremely buttered spinach" **Alastair Little**
"Mouthwatering" **Janet Street-Porter**

DESSERT
Baked Apple Sponge with Brandy Cream

PORK FILLET IN RICH ONION AND MADEIRA SAUCE

1 pork fillet (tenderloin), about 350 g
   (12 oz)
30 ml (2 tbsp) olive oil
1 onion, finely chopped
1 fat clove garlic, crushed
handful of thyme leaves
1 vegetable stock cube, dissolved in
   300 ml (½ pint) boiling water
5 ml (1 tsp) Dijon mustard
5 ml (1 tsp) tomato purée
30 ml (2 tbsp) Madeira
salt and freshly ground black pepper
50 g (2 oz) button mushrooms
7.5 ml (1½ tsp) cornflour
milk if necessary

Marinade:
30 ml (2 tbsp) extra-virgin olive oil
5 ml (1 tsp) golden syrup
4 spring onions, chopped
15 ml (1 tbsp) chopped parsley
1 rosemary sprig
5 ml (1 tsp) thyme leaves
juice of ¼ lemon

1 Split the pork fillet lengthways and cut any membrane and fat away. Place the pieces of pork in a glass dish. Mix the marinade ingredients together and pour over the pork. Leave overnight in the refrigerator.

2 Preheat the oven to 200°C (400°F) mark 6, and put a casserole dish in the oven to warm.

3 Remove the pork from the marinade and pat dry. Heat the olive oil in a frying pan, add the pork and fry quickly over a high heat, turning to seal and brown on all sides. Transfer to the warmed casserole dish.

4 Fry the onion gently in the fat remaining in the frying pan to soften. Add the garlic and thyme leaves, and fry for 1 minute. Add the stock, mustard, tomato purée, Madeira and black pepper to taste. Bring to the boil, lower the heat and simmer for 2-3 minutes.

5 Add the sauce to the meat in the casserole, mix well, then cover with foil. Cook in a preheated oven for 30 minutes.

6 Add the button mushrooms to the casserole and stir in. Return to the oven for 15 minutes.

7 Mix the cornflour with a little milk or water, and stir into the casserole. Taste for seasoning.

8 Return to the oven for at least another 15 minutes.

9 To serve, slice the pork and fan out on warmed serving plates. Pour on the sauce and serve with the Spinach Nests (see right).

COOK'S TIP

This is a good dish to leave in the oven for quite a lot longer if needed. Just keep checking the amount of liquid and add a little milk if the sauce is getting too thick.

SPINACH NESTS FILLED WITH MUSHROOMS AND BACON IN CREAM

450 g (1 lb) spinach, cleaned
50-75 g (2-3 oz) butter
2 rashers streaky bacon
50 g (2 oz) button mushrooms, sliced
a generous 5 ml (1 tsp) double cream
freshly ground black pepper

1 Melt 50 g (2 oz) of the butter in a saucepan and add the spinach. Stir until the spinach is reduced in volume, about 3-4 minutes.

2 Transfer the spinach to a colander and press well down with a potato masher to remove most of the moisture. Place the spinach on a paper towel to absorb the excess butter. Leave to cool.

3 Chop the bacon into small pieces and fry in the remaining butter until nearly crisp. Add the mushrooms and fry until just cooked. Add the cream and pepper to taste.

4 Cut 4 small pieces of foil and shape nests of spinach within the foil, using your fingers. (Yes, this is the messy bit!) Spoon the mushrooms and bacon into the middle.

5 Fold down the foil and reheat in the oven at 200°C (400°F) mark 6 for about 10 minutes. Transfer the spinach nests, using a spatula or fish slice, to the warmed serving plates, leaving the foil shapes behind.

BAKED APPLE SPONGE WITH BRANDY CREAM

2 Bramley cooking apples
60 g (2¼ oz) soft margarine
a little brown sugar
good pinch of ground cinnamon
50 g (2 oz) caster sugar
1 egg
125 g (4 oz) self-raising flour
dash of milk

Brandy Cream:
60 ml (2 fl oz) double cream
5 ml (1 tsp) caster sugar
10 ml (2 tsp) brandy

1 Preheat the oven to 200°C (400°F) mark 6. Use a little of the margarine to grease 4 individual metal pudding basins.

2 Peel the apples and slice small chunks of them into the pudding basins. Sprinkle with brown sugar and a good pinch of cinnamon.

3 Cream the sugar and remaining margarine together in a bowl until light and fluffy. Beat in the egg. Fold in the flour and a little milk, to make a fairly stiff mixture. (This can be done with an electric hand mixer.)

4 Put a good spoonful of the sponge mixture on top of each portion of apples, spreading it over roughly. Bake in the middle of the oven for about 30 minutes.

5 To prepare the brandy cream, whip the cream, with the caster sugar and brandy.

6 To serve, turn the apple sponges out onto warmed individual serving plates and accompany with the brandy cream.

Note: This recipe serves 4.

The Third Semi-Final

Graham Booth's Menu

MAIN COURSE
Glazed Noisettes of Lamb with Apricot Stuffing
Rösti Potatoes with a hint of Ginger
French Beans with Radicchio
"Absolutely excellent" **Alastair Little**
"Better than I would ever achieve in the time scale" **Janet Street-Porter**

DESSERT
White Chocolate Silk with Raspberry Coulis

GLAZED NOISETTES OF LAMB WITH APRICOT STUFFING

1 best end of lamb, 6-7 cutlets
225 ml (7½ fl oz) medium dry white
  wine
salt and freshly ground black pepper
30 ml (2 tbsp) crabapple or similar jelly

Apricot Stuffing:
125 g (4 oz) dried apricots
50 g (2 oz) sultanas
15 ml (1 tbsp) chopped parsley
15 ml (1 tbsp) chopped mint

Glaze:
30 ml (2 tbsp) clear honey
30 ml (2 tbsp) French mustard

To Garnish:
chopped parsley

1 Ask the butcher to remove the bone from the best end, and strip off the outer skin of the lamb. The butcher will also prepare the string for tying and leave it loose in 6-7 separate sections.

2 For the stuffing, chop the apricots, sultanas, parsley and mint and mix together. Season with salt and pepper. For the glaze, mix the honey and mustard together, and spread half of this on the inside of the lamb. Spread with the apricot stuffing and roll up carefully, tightening the strings at regular intervals. Spread the remaining glaze over the outer side of the lamb.

3 Place the lamb on a roasting rack in a roasting tin and pour a little of the wine into the tin. Cook in a preheated oven at 220°C (425°F) mark 7 for 40 minutes.

4 When cooked, remove the lamb from the oven, cover and leave to rest in a warm place while preparing the sauce. Place the roasting tin on the hob and simmer the juices remaining in the tin to reduce. Add the remaining wine and crabapple jelly; stir until smooth and thoroughly heated through.

5 Carve the lamb into noisettes and arrange on warmed serving plates. Garnish with the chopped parsley and serve with the sauce.

COOK'S TIP

You could include 6-8 button onions as an extra garnish. Peel the onions and par-boil in salted water for 10 minutes. Drain and cook in the roasting tin with the lamb.

RÖSTI POTATOES WITH A HINT OF GINGER

175-225 g (6-8 oz) even-sized
  potatoes, scrubbed
grated fresh root ginger, to taste
salt and freshly ground black pepper
30 ml (2 tbsp) oil

1 Cook the potatoes in their skins in a pan of boiling water for 10 minutes. Drain and peel while still warm, then leave to cool.

2 Coarsely grate the cooled potatoes into a bowl, and add the ginger and seasoning to taste.

3 Heat the oil in a large frying pan. Spoon the potato mixture into 2 biscuit cutters, 5-7.5 cm (2-3 inches) in diameter, and press down well. Lift on to a spatula and place carefully in the frying pan. Cook over a medium heat until brown on the undersides, about 10 minutes. Turn the cutters carefully, pressing the mixture down again if necessary. Cook for a further 10 minutes until golden brown.

4 Lift the rösti out of the pan, using a fish slice, and carefully remove the cutters. Serve the rösti piping hot.

FRENCH BEANS WITH RADICCHIO

250 g (9 oz) French beans, trimmed
salt
25 g (1 oz) butter
1 small radicchio heart, washed and
  shredded
1 sugar lump

1 Bring enough water to the boil in a saucepan to just cover the beans. Add the salt and butter, then add the beans. Boil for 4-5 minutes.

2 Add the radicchio and sugar lump to the beans 1 minute before the end of the cooking time.

3 Drain and serve at once.

WHITE CHOCOLATE SILK WITH RASPBERRY COULIS

7.5 ml (½ tsp) powdered gelatine
25 ml (1 fl oz) cold water
125 ml (4 fl oz) milk
2 egg yolks
45 g (1¾ oz) sugar
100 g (3½ oz) white chocolate, grated
25 ml (1 fl oz) Malibu liqueur
1 egg white
175 ml (6 fl oz) double cream

Raspberry Coulis:
225 g (8 oz) fresh raspberries
45 ml (3 tbsp) icing sugar

To Decorate:
desiccated coconut

1 Sprinkle the gelatine on to the cold water in a small bowl and leave until softened and sponge-like. Warm the milk in a saucepan to boiling point. Beat the egg yolks with the sugar in a bowl, then add a little of the hot milk. Pour this mixture back into the hot milk. Stir over a gentle heat until the custard is cooked and thickened enough to coat the back of the spoon; do not allow to boil.

2 Pour the gelatine into the hot custard, stirring to dissolve it, then add the grated white chocolate. Stir until the chocolate has melted, to form a smooth, creamy mixture. Add the Malibu. Allow to partially set in the refrigerator.

3 Grease 4 individual moulds with a little butter. Whip the egg white to a firm peak stage. Whip the cream and fold it into the egg white. Fold this into the chocolate mixture, then pour into the greased moulds. Leave to set in the refrigerator overnight.

4 For the coulis, put the raspberries and icing sugar into a blender or food processor and process until smooth, then pass through a nylon sieve to get rid of the seeds. Chill.

5 To serve, loosen the puddings from the sides of the moulds with a knife dipped in hot water (or the handle of a teaspoon if the moulds are fluted). Turn the puddings out on to serving plates and surround with the raspberry coulis. Sprinkle with a little desiccated coconut to decorate.

Note: This recipe makes 4.

The Third Semi-Final

Miranda Tetley • Graham Booth • Gaia Skibinski

Panel of Judges
Alastair Little • Janet Street-Porter • Loyd Grossman

Gaia Skibinski's Menu

MAIN COURSE
Pheasant Breast with Chestnut Tagliatelle and Mushroom Sauce
"All the tastes together were excellent" **Janet Street-Porter**
Mixed Leaf Salad

DESSERT
Passion Fruit Mousse with Passion Fruit Sauce
"A perfect passion fruit" **Loyd**

PHEASANT BREAST WITH CHESTNUT TAGLIATELLE AND MUSHROOM SAUCE

2 pheasant breasts, skinned (carcass reserved for the stock)
about 30 ml (2 tbsp) olive oil
25 g (1 oz) butter
salt and freshly ground black pepper

Mushroom Sauce:
25 g (1 oz) porcini (dried mushrooms)
15 ml (1 tbsp) olive oil
¼ onion, chopped
75 g (3 oz) field mushrooms, chopped
game stock (see below)
60 ml (2 fl oz) double cream
15 ml (1 tbsp) chopped flat-leaf parsley

Chestnut Pasta:
50 g (2 oz) chestnut flour
75 g (3 oz) pasta flour (type '00')
1 egg

1 Brush the pheasant with the olive oil and leave to marinate in the refrigerator overnight.

2 Prepare the porcini for the sauce. Soak in warm water for 20 minutes, then drain, reserving the liquid, and chop.

3 Make the pasta. Mix the two flours together and make a well in the centre. Add the egg and a little salt, and mix and knead to a smooth dough. Put in a plastic bag and leave to rest for 20 minutes. Pass the dough through a pasta machine repeatedly, gradually narrowing the setting until the pasta is very thin. Cut the sheets of pasta into 1 cm (½ inch) wide strips, with a pasta cutter. Drape over a clean tea towel and leave to dry for 5-10 minutes.

4 Heat the butter in a frying pan and fry the pheasant breasts on both sides until lightly browned. Season with salt and pepper and transfer to a baking tin. Roast in a preheated oven at 220°C (425°F) mark 7 for 10 minutes. Remove from the oven and keep warm.

5 Meanwhile make the mushroom sauce. Heat the olive oil in a pan, add the onion and cook until softened. Add the porcini, fresh mushrooms and the porcini liquid. Fry, stirring, for 1-2 minutes. Add the game stock and leave to cook over high heat until the stock is reduced to a syrup. Season with salt and pepper. Stir in the cream and chopped parsley.

6 Cook the pasta in plenty of boiling salted water until *al dente*, (tender but firm to the bite), then drain.

7 To serve, place a pheasant breast on each warmed serving plate and pour on some of the mushroom sauce. Add the remaining sauce to the chestnut pasta and toss to mix. Divide between the serving plates. Serve accompanied by a leafy salad dressed with oil and vinegar.

GAME STOCK

Cut the pheasant carcass into pieces and put in a roasting tin in the preheated oven at 220°C (425°F) mark 7. After 15 minutes, remove from the oven and pour off the fat. Transfer the carcass to a saucepan and add 30 ml (2 tbsp) Cognac;1 onion, chopped; 1 carrot, chopped; 1 leek, chopped; a bouquet garni, few black peppercorns and a few juniper berries. Add sufficient cold water to cover, bring to the boil, skim, then lower the heat and simmer, uncovered, for 1 hour. Strain. Season to taste with salt.

PASSION FRUIT MOUSSE WITH PASSION FRUIT SAUCE

2 gelatine leaves
11 passion fruit
juice of 1 orange
50 g (2 oz) caster sugar
60 ml (2 fl oz) whipping cream
1 egg white

Passion Fruit Sauce:
7 passion fruit
juice of ½ orange
35 g (1¼ oz) icing sugar

1 Put the gelatine leaves into a bowl of cold water and leave to soften, then squeeze to remove excess moisture.

2 Halve the passion fruit and scoop out the pulp and seeds into a nylon sieve over a bowl. Press the pulp through, then sieve the orange juice into the bowl. Measure the juice: you should have 175 ml (6 fl oz). Pour into a saucepan and add the sugar and gelatine leaves. Dissolve over a low heat, then leave to cool.

3 Whip the cream until thick. In a separate bowl, whisk the egg white until soft peaks form.

4 Once the passion fruit mixture has cooled, fold it into the whipped cream, followed by the whisked egg white. Pour into chilled glasses and put into the refrigerator to set.

5 To prepare the passion fruit sauce, halve six of the passion fruit and scoop out the pulp and seeds into a nylon sieve over a pan. Press the pulp through, add the orange juice and icing sugar and dissolve over a low heat. Bring the mixture to the boil and boil until it becomes syrup-like, then take off the heat and allow to cool. Add the pulp and seeds of the remaining passion fruit and mix well.

6 When the mousses have set, take out of the refrigerator and pour the passion fruit sauce on top to serve.

The Final

Contestants
Camilla Askaroff • Katie Targett-Adams • Miranda Tetley

Panel of Judges
Michel Roux • Sir John Harvey-Jones • Loyd Grossman

WINNER

Camilla Askaroff's Menu

MAIN COURSE
Pork Tenderloin with a Surprise Stuffing on a Beetroot Sauce
Potato, Carrot and Turnip Röstis
Rocket Salad with a Lime and Sherry Vinegar Dressing
"Beautifully cooked, very moist" **Michel Roux**

DESSERT
Steamed Apricot Puddings with an Apricot and Pistachio
Butterscotch Sauce and Amaretto Cream
"A wonderful, delicious steamed pudding" **Loyd**

TENDERLOIN OF PORK WITH A SURPRISE STUFFING ON A BEETROOT SAUCE

1 pork tenderloin
about 30 ml (2 tbsp) olive oil
6 shallots
150 ml (¼ pint) white wine

Stuffing:
125 g (4 oz) spinach, steamed for 4
    minutes and chopped
1 clove garlic, crushed
1 spring onion, chopped
25 g (1 oz) cooked smoked ham,
    chopped
15 ml (1 tbsp) pine nuts
3 sun-dried tomatoes, sliced
15 ml (1 tbsp) freshly grated Parmesan
    cheese
lots of freshly ground black pepper
15 ml (1 tbsp) oil from sun-dried
    tomatoes

Sauce:
600 ml (1 pint) homemade ham stock
3 cooked beetroot
3 bay leaves
5 ml (1 tsp) cloves
squeeze of lemon juice
50 g (2 oz) butter
15 ml (1 tbsp) plain flour

To Garnish:
flat-leaf parsley

1 The day before serving, bring the ham stock to simmering point. Remove from the heat and add two of the cooked beetroots cut into chunks, the bay leaves, cloves and lemon juice. Leave to infuse for 24 hours to extract flavour and colour from the beetroots.

2 The next day, strain the stock and discard beetroot, spices and bay leaves.

3 To make the stuffing, mix all the ingredients together, binding the mixture with the oil from the sun-dried tomatoes.

4 Cut the pork tenderloin in half width-ways and slit each piece lengthways, but do not cut right through. Open out each piece like a book and spread with the stuffing. Fold over to enclose and tie securely at intervals with string.

5 Heat the olive oil in a sauté pan with a lid, add the shallots and sauté until browned. Add both pieces of meat and seal on all sides. Add the white wine, bring to the boil, then simmer, covered, for 20 minutes, turning once.

6 Meanwhile make the sauce. Bring the strained stock to the boil. Knead the butter with the flour to make a beurre manié. Whisk the beurre manie into the stock a little at a time, adding just enough to thicken the sauce.

7 Cut half of the remaining cooked beetroot into thin strips for the garnish; cut the other half into a few rough chunks. Stir the latter into the sauce to add colour.

8 To serve, carve each piece of meat into about 5 slices. Strain the sauce and pool some on to each warmed serving plate. Place the slices of meat on top of the sauce, and arrange the shallots and beetroot around. Garnish with parsley and serve with the accompaniments.

POTATO, CARROT AND TURNIP RÖSTIS

1 small turnip
1 carrot
2 potatoes, about 225 g (8 oz) total
    weight
1 clove garlic, crushed
salt and freshly ground black pepper
about 30 ml (2 tbsp) olive oil

1 Peel the turnip, carrot and potatoes. Place in a pan, cover with cold water, bring to the boil and simmer for 8 minutes. Remove the turnip after 4 minutes. Drain and leave to cool.

2 Grate the vegetables coarsely and place in a bowl with the garlic, salt and pepper. Use 2 forks to mix the ingredients, to distribute colour and flavour evenly. Divide the mixture into 4 portions and shape into flat cakes, using your hands, squeezing well to stick the mixture together. Set aside until ready to cook.

3 Heat the olive oil in a frying pan, add the vegetable cakes and fry over a moderate heat for about 3 minutes on each side, until crisp and golden, adding more oil as necessary. Drain on kitchen paper and serve.

ROCKET SALAD WITH A LIME AND SHERRY VINEGAR DRESSING

selection of salad leaves (preferably
    mainly rocket, with chicory and red-
    leaved lettuce)
few flat-leaf parsley sprigs
few tarragon sprigs

Dressing:
15 ml (1 tbsp) sherry vinegar
30 ml (2 tbsp) extra-virgin olive oil
5 ml (1 tsp) Dijon mustard
1 drop of lime oil
freshly ground black pepper
2.5 ml (½ tsp) tomato purée

Croûtons:
1 slice Granary bread
olive oil, for shallow frying

To Serve:
freshly pared Parmesan cheese

1 For the dressing, mix all the ingredients together in a screw-topped jar and shake well to combine.

2 To make the croûtons, remove the crusts from the bread and cut into little squares. Heat the olive oil in a small frying pan, add the bread squares and fry, turning, until brown and crisp. Drain well on kitchen paper.

3 Arrange the salad and herb leaves on individual plates and pour over the dressing evenly. Sprinkle with the croûtons and some shavings of Parmesan.

LIME OIL

Like other citrus oils, lime is extracted from the rind of the fruit and has a very strong flavour. A drop is all that is required to impart the flavour and aroma to this dressing.

THE FINAL

STEAMED APRICOT PUDDINGS WITH AN APRICOT AND PISTACHIO BUTTERSCOTCH SAUCE AND AMARETTO CREAM

75 g (3 oz) fresh apricots, stoned and chopped
90 ml (3 fl oz) boiling water
2.5 ml (½ tsp) bicarbonate of soda
40 g (1½ oz) butter
65 g (2½ oz) caster sugar
75 g (3 oz) self-raising flour

Sauce:
75 g (3 oz) fresh apricots, stoned and chopped
15 g (½ oz) pistachio nuts, chopped
50 g (2 oz) butter
30 ml (2 tbsp) brown sugar
45 - 60 ml (3 - 4 tbsp) double cream

Amaretto Cream:
150 ml (¼ pint) double cream
30 ml (2 tbsp) amaretto di Saronno liqueur

To Serve:
icing sugar, for dusting
ground cinnamon

1 For the puddings, in a bowl mix the apricots with the boiling water and bicarbonate of soda. In another bowl, cream the butter and sugar together, then fold in the flour and the apricot mixture. Put into greased 150 ml (¼ pint) individual metal pudding basins to two-thirds fill, and cover with greased foil. Steam for 30 minutes.

2 To make the sauce, mix the apricots, pistachios, butter and sugar together in a small pan. Stir over a low heat until the butter is melted and the sugar is dissolved. When the mixture starts to boil, add just enough double cream to make a light brown butterscotch sauce. Make sure the sauce isn't too runny, and don't overheat.

3 To make the amaretto cream, whip the cream until thick, then fold in the liqueur. Chill before serving.

4 To serve, dust each serving plate with icing sugar. Turn the puddings out of the basins on to the plates. Pour the warm sauce over the puddings, and place a dollop of cream next to each one. Sprinkle a little cinnamon over the cream. Serve at once.

The Final

Contestants

Camilla Askaroff • Katie Targett-Adams • Miranda Tetley

Panel of Judges

Michel Roux • Sir John Harvey-Jones • Loyd Grossman

Katie Targett-Adams' Menu

MAIN COURSE

Roulade of Monkfish and Bacon on a bed of Potato, Leek and Asparagus, served with a Sweet Pepper Sauce

Tomato and Courgette Tapas

"Sensational sweet pepper sauce" **Sir John Harvey-Jones**

DESSERT

Brioche and Date Pudding, with Toffee Sauce

Crème Ecossaise

"Lovely dessert, excellent... I loved that pudding" **Michel Roux**

ROULADE OF MONKFISH AND BACON ON A BED OF POTATO, LEEK AND ASPARAGUS

2 pieces of monkfish fillet, each about
    175 g (6 oz) and 25 cm (10 inches)
    long
6 strips unsmoked streaky bacon
10 Roseval potatoes (or any pink or
    new potatoes)
1 leek, white part only, washed
14 medium asparagus spears
about 30 ml (2 tbsp) virgin olive oil
salt and freshly ground white pepper

Sweet Yellow Pepper Sauce:
15 ml (1 tbsp) olive oil
2 small cloves garlic, crushed
1 shallot, diced
2 yellow peppers, cored, deseeded and
    diced
2 thyme sprigs
300 ml (½ pint) fish stock
60 ml (2 fl oz) double cream

To Serve:
lamb's lettuce or watercress

1 Make the sauce first. Heat the olive oil in a frying pan, add the garlic and shallot and cook gently until transparent. Add the pepper dice, thyme, stock and salt and pepper to taste. Bring to the boil, then lower the heat and simmer for about 20 minutes. Purée the mixture in a blender or food processor, then add the cream. Set aside.

2 Stretch the bacon strips with the blunt edge of a knife until half their length again. Arrange each of the monkfish strips in a circle and carefully wrap the bacon over and over the fish until completely covered, taking care not to overlap the bacon. Secure with cocktail sticks. Repeat with the other fillet.

3 Put the bacon-wrapped monkfish on a foil-lined baking tray. Cook in a preheated oven at 180°C (350°F) mark 4, for 20 minutes, or until the bacon is cooked and the fish flakes easily. Check the fish occasionally, turning if necessary; don't let the bacon become too crispy and well done.

4 Meanwhile, slice the potatoes into thin discs. Cook in boiling salted water for about 8 minutes until al dente (tender, but firm to the bite). Drain thoroughly.

5 Cut the leek into 2.5 cm (1 inch) lengths. Take one of these lengths and slice lengthways in half. Discard the central layers and retain the outer larger squares. Repeat with the rest of the leek.

6 Cut the top 5 cm (2 inches) from each asparagus spear; steam these asparagus tips for 5 minutes or until tender. (Use the rest of the asparagus for another dish.)

7 Meanwhile, heat the oil in a large frying pan, add the potato slices and fry gently, turning occasionally, for a few minutes. Add the leek and cook for 1 minute. Season with salt and pepper to taste. Add 4-6 asparagus tips and toss gently to heat through, being careful not to break the asparagus.

8 When ready to serve, gently reheat the sauce. Remove the cocktail sticks from the fish. Divide the stir-fry between the warmed serving plates and top each portion with a monkfish roulade. Position the reserved asparagus tips pointing outwards from the middle of the roulade and arrange a small handful of lamb's lettuce in the centre of the fish. Serve with the sweet pepper sauce, and tomato and courgette tapas.

TOMATO AND COURGETTE TAPAS

2 courgettes
15 ml (1 tbsp) virgin olive oil
6 small red tomatoes
salt and freshly ground black pepper
freshly grated nutmeg
15 ml (1 tbsp) double cream

1 Cut the courgettes into thin slices. Heat the olive oil in a pan and fry the courgette slices until tender, not letting them brown too much.

2 Cut the lids off the tomatoes and reserve. Scoop out the seeds with a teaspoon. Cut a fine slice off the bottom of each tomato, but do not pierce right through the flesh. This enables the tomatoes to stand upright.

3 Season the courgette and sprinkle with nutmeg to taste. Purée in a blender or food processor and add the cream.

4 Fill the tomatoes with the courgette mixture, piling it up well. Replace the tomato lids. (The filling should be visible under the lids.)

5 Place the stuffed tomatoes on a baking tray and warm through in a preheated oven at 180°C (350°F) mark 4 for 5 minutes. Serve.

BRIOCHE AND DATE PUDDING WITH TOFFEE SAUCE

4 brioches
50 g (2 oz) butter, melted
2 eggs
40 g (1½ oz) caster sugar
300 ml (½ pint) milk
5 ml (1 tsp) vanilla essence
5 ml (1 tsp) ground cinnamon
6 fresh dates, stoned and chopped
15 ml (1 tbsp) muscovado sugar

Toffee Sauce:
7.5 ml (½ tbsp) butter
30 ml (2 tbsp) light muscovado sugar
5 ml (1 tsp) vanilla essence
150 ml (¼ pint) double cream

To Serve:
icing sugar, for dusting
Crème Ecossaise (see right)

1 Break the brioches up into pieces and soak them in the melted butter. Place on a baking tray and put in a preheated oven at 170°C (340°F) mark 3-4 until crispy, about 10 minutes.

2 Beat the eggs and sugar together in a bowl, then gradually stir in the milk, vanilla essence and cinnamon.

3 Add the chopped dates and brioche pieces to the custard mixture, and spoon into individual greased ramekins. Sprinkle with muscovado sugar.

4 Stand the ramekins in a roasting tin containing enough hot water to come halfway up the sides of the dishes. Bake in the oven for about 30 minutes until firm.

5 To make the sauce, melt the butter with the sugar in a small saucepan over a low heat. Add the vanilla essence and cream. Stir until thoroughly mixed and the sugar has dissolved. Bring to the boil, and take off the heat. When ready to serve, heat through gently.

6 To serve, turn the puddings out of the ramekins onto warmed serving plates and dust with icing sugar. Serve with the warm toffee sauce and cold crème Ecossaise.

Note: This recipe makes 4 puddings.

CREME ECOSSAISE

75 ml (2½ fl oz) milk
75 ml (2½ fl oz) double cream
30 ml (2 tbsp) whisky
25 g (1 oz) caster sugar
2 egg yolks

1 Place the milk, cream and whisky in a pan. Bring to the boil and remove from the heat immediately. Leave to infuse.

2 Meanwhile, place the sugar and egg yolks in a bowl and beat with an electric hand whisk until pale and creamy. Add slowly to the whisky mixture, stirring all the time. Place on a gentle heat, and continue to stir until the sauce thickens. Allow to cool.

3 Pass through a sieve into a bowl. Cover and place in the refrigerator until needed. Serve with the brioche and date pudding.

The Final

Contestants

Camilla Askaroff • Katie Targett-Adams • Miranda Tetley

Panel of Judges

Michel Roux • Sir John Harvey-Jones • Loyd Grossman

Miranda Tetley's Menu

MAIN COURSE

Stuffed Tenderloin of Pork roasted with Shallots, served with a Soured Cream Sauce

Baby New Potatoes

Buttered Beetroots

Sautéed Broccoli

"Moist pork and very pleasant stuffing" **Michel Roux**

DESSERT

Apple and Mincemeat with a Brown Meringue Topping

"Superb... absolutely beautifully done" **Sir John Harvey-Jones**

STUFFED TENDERLOIN OF PORK ROASTED WITH SHALLOTS, SERVED WITH A SOURED CREAM SAUCE

1 fillet of pork, about 350 g (12 oz)
salt and freshly ground black pepper
15 ml (1 tbsp) olive oil
25 g (1 oz) butter, softened
5 ml (1 tsp) fresh thyme leaves
8 shallots

Marinade:
30 ml (2 tbsp) olive oil
juice of ½ lemon
3-4 spring onions, finely chopped

Stuffing:
25 g (1 oz) butter
½ small onion, diced
10 ml (2 tsp) thyme leaves
10 ml (2 tsp) chopped parsley
6 button mushrooms, sliced
6 pistachio nuts, chopped
25 g (1 oz) sultanas
1 small slice Granary bread, made into
    breadcrumbs
grated rind of 1 lemon

Sauce:
25 g (1 oz) butter
½ small onion, diced
4 organic brown mushrooms, sliced
150 ml (¼ pint) soured cream

1 Trim the pork fillet and place in a dish. Mix the marinade ingredients together and pour over the pork. Cover and leave to marinate overnight in the refrigerator.

2 To make the stuffing, melt the butter in a frying pan, add the onion, thyme and parsley, and fry, stirring, for a few minutes. Add the remaining stuffing ingredients, plus salt and pepper to taste, and stir together. Transfer to a bowl and leave to cool for 1 minute.

3 Slit the pork fillet lengthwise, without cutting right through. Open out, like a book, and season well on the inside. Place the stuffing along one half of the meat, then fold the other half over to enclose and secure with wooden cocktail sticks.

4 Heat the olive oil in a frying pan, add the pork fillet and seal quickly on all sides over a high heat. Transfer to a heated roasting tin and smear with the butter. Sprinkle with the thyme leaves, then put into the middle of a preheated oven at 200°C (400°F) mark 6. Cook for 1 hour, basting fairly frequently, adding the shallots to the tin halfway through cooking.

5 To make the sauce, melt the butter in a pan and fry the onion gently to soften and brown lightly. Add the mushrooms and fry for 2-3 minutes until softened. Add the soured cream and salt and pepper to taste. Warm through; do not boil.

6 To serve, slice the pork and fan out on warmed serving plates. Add the shallots and serve with the soured cream sauce.

APPLE AND MINCEMEAT WITH A BROWN MERINGUE TOPPING

2 small Bramley cooking apples
good pinch of ground cinnamon
about 15 ml (1 tbsp) good-quality
  mincemeat
2 egg whites
50 g (2 oz) fine soft brown sugar
5 ml (1 tsp) white wine vinegar

To Serve:
single cream

1 Preheat the oven to 200°C (400°F) mark 6 and butter 2 individual metal pudding basins.

2 Peel and slice the apples, then put in a small saucepan with a little water and the cinnamon. Cook quickly to soften just a little.

3 Two-thirds fill each pudding basin with apple, add the mincemeat and stir to mix.

4 In a bowl, whisk the egg whites until they form stiff peaks. Whisk in the brown sugar, one third at a time, together with the vinegar. Don't over-whisk.

5 Dollop the meringue on top of the apple mixture, then cook in the middle of the preheated oven for 15-20 minutes. Turn out of the pudding basins on to warmed serving plates and serve with single cream.

INDEX

OF RECIPE TITLES AND CONTESTANTS